*THE*

# QUEEN

### A CELEBRATION OF
### 40 GLORIOUS
### YEARS

# THE
# QUEEN

## A CELEBRATION OF
## 40 GLORIOUS
## YEARS

JANICE ANDERSON

IN ASSOCIATION WITH THE
HULTON PICTURE COMPANY

by the Endeavour Group, UK
85 Larkhill Rise
London SW4 6HR

© 1992 The Endeavour Group, UK

ISBN 1 873 913 001

Printed in Italy
by G. Canale & C. S.p.A. - Borgaro T.se - Torino

# CONTENTS

# The Years of Preparation
## 1926–1952

ABOVE: *Princess Elizabeth of York, aged two.*
RIGHT: *The Duke and Duchess of York with their baby daughter.*

ELIZABETH II HAS BEEN 'BY the grace of God of the United Kingdom of Great Britain and Northern Ireland and of Her other Realms and Territories Queen, Head of the Commonwealth, Defender of the Faith' for 40 years. She is the 40th Monarch to have sat on the English throne since her ancestor William the Conqueror snatched it from the last Anglo-Saxon king, Harold II, from whom she is also descended. In the Scottish monarchy, she is 13th in descent from Mary Queen of Scots and 22nd from Robert the Bruce. Of the kings and queens who have preceded her, only six have reigned longer than she has.

It is a splendid heritage. And it is one to which the baby girl born to George V's second son, Albert, Duke of York and his charming Duchess at 27 Bruton Street in London on 21 April 1926, seemed to have little chance of succeeding. After all, there was a Prince of Wales (Albert's handsome and popular brother David) ready to succeed their father, and it was likely that the Yorks would themselves have a son, who would automatically supplant his sister in the order of succession.

Despite this, the baby's birth aroused considerable interest—much more than had been shown in George V's two other grandchildren, the sons of his daughter Mary (later the Princess Royal). It was an interest which never diminished.

*'What a tremendous joy it is . . . .*
*to have our little girl . . . .'*

LEFT: *Lilibet and her nurse 'Allah' (Mrs Clara Knight) leaving for Christmas at Sandringham, 1929.*

BELOW: *The little Welsh house was presented to Princess Elizabeth by the people of Wales to mark her sixth birthday. It is still at Royal Lodge, Windsor, still delighting later generations of royal children.*

RIGHT: *A charming, carefree study of the Duchess of York and her two daughters: it is summer 1936, and already midway through Edward VIII's brief reign. The Duchess will be Queen before the year is out, and the Princess Elizabeth, Heir Presumptive.*

The first glimpse anyone outside the royal circle had of the baby was in the official photograph taken at the time of her christening, an occasion surrounded by the rich trappings of the baby's royal heritage. It took place a month after her birth in the private chapel at Buckingham Palace, and she was christened Elizabeth Alexandra Mary, after her mother, great grandmother and grandmother. The baptism was performed by the Archbishop of York, using Jordan water from the Holy Land held in a gold lily-shaped font which had been designed by Prince Albert. The Honiton lace robe which enveloped the baby had been made for Queen Victoria's children.

The baby's parents doted on her, and were much more closely and affectionately involved with her upbringing than George V and Queen Mary had been in their children's. Perhaps mellowed by the passing of time, King George adored his granddaughter. When the Duke and Duchess of York left England in January 1927 for a six-month world tour, the baby was left in the care of both her sets of grandparents, spending as much time with the Duke of York's mother and father as with the Earl and Countess of Strathmore, the Duchess of York's parents.

### VIEW FROM THE BALCONY

The Yorks' return to England in June allowed the world its first glimpse of the baby Elizabeth, now a curly-haired toddler as, held in her mother's arms, she watched from the balcony of Buckingham Palace the vast crowds which had gathered to welcome home the royal travellers. Queen Mary was there, holding an umbrella over mother and child, and George V beamed benevolently in the background.

Now began an idyllic childhood for the little princess. It was centred on two houses, the Yorks' London home at 145 Piccadilly, a great four-storey mansion near Hyde Park Corner into which they moved in 1927, and, from early 1932, a 'country house'—Royal Lodge in Windsor Great Park. Caring for the royal child in both houses was a nurse, Mrs Clara Knight, who had been the Duchess of York's nurse, and a young Scottish

nursery maid, Margaret MacDonald, who remains Elizabeth II's dresser and close confidante to this day.

Their charge was an enchantingly pretty little girl, as the celebrated photographs taken of her by Marcus Adams at 145 Piccadilly in July 1928, demonstrated. Postcards of these pictures were enthusiastically collected by people everywhere and aroused tremendous interest in her.

She was also very bright and quick-witted, with neat nicknames for everyone whose names were too difficult for her childish tongue—'Allah' for Clara Knight, 'Bobo' for Margaret MacDonald, and 'Lilibet' for herself. The last nickname was very soon accepted as the Royal Family's name for her; even Queen Mary used it, noting in her diary in March 1929, for instance, 'I played with Lilibet in the garden making sand pies!' The garden was at Bognor, where George V was recovering from an abscess in his lung which had very nearly killed him, and to where his little granddaughter had been brought as the perfect tonic to aid his recovery.

From August 1930, the princess had a new sister to share her nursery and her childhood—and to be provided with a nickname. 'I shall call her Bud,' said the four-year-old Lilibet, looking down at the baby Margaret Rose in her cradle.

Little upset the quiet tenor of the York family's life in the early 1930s. For the children especially, the great industrial depression of the time, which meant unemployment for millions, was something beyond their understanding. Lilibet was learning to read and write, and to ride—her favourite thing. The princess was only two and a half when she had her first riding lessons and was given her first pony for her third birthday by her royal grandfather.

By the time the princess's formal education began at the age of six, many toy horses lined the corridor outside her bedroom and were carefully unsaddled and put to bed every night. The new governess, Miss Marion Crawford—'Crawfie' to the princesses and to the millions of readers of the books she published after her 17 years in the royal schoolroom—had her first glimpse of her new charge sitting up in bed giving her horses a last drive round the park before settling down to sleep. It was all perfect. Even the lessons in the early years were hardly burdensome—less than two hours in the mornings devoted to the three Rs, with afternoons being time for music, dancing, singing, drawing and learning to swim at the Bath Club.

## ABDICATION

In January 1936, Lilibet's 'very very kind' grandpapa George V died, and was succeeded by his son David, who became king as Edward VIII.

LEFT: *Presenting a united front after the trauma of the Abdication, the Royal Family waves from the balcony at Buckingham Palace after George VI's coronation.*

BELOW: *Elizabeth and Margaret on an outing with their governess, 'Crawfie'. They are visiting the YWCA in London after a trip on the Underground.*

RIGHT: *Elizabeth (front, left) ready to try for a life-saving award at the Bath Club, London in 1939. She and Margaret both learned to swim here.*

The whisperings about Uncle David's private life, especially his obsession with a divorced woman, Mrs Wallis Simpson, may not have reached the royal nursery, but they were certainly known to the Duke and Duchess of York and Queen Mary. By December, what had seemed totally unthinkable less than a year before, had happened: Edward VIII, unable to persuade anyone that Mrs Simpson could become a suitable wife and queen, and equally unable to remain king without her, abdicated.

On 11 December 1936, the Instrument of Abdication, which had been signed and witnessed the day before by all four of George V's sons, was ratified by Parliament, and the Duke of York became king, taking the name of George VI. His daughter Elizabeth was Heir Presumptive to the throne, 'presumptive' because there might still be a son born to the new king and queen.

The Yorks, now head and heart of the Royal Family, moved into Buckingham Palace and plans for the king's coronation went ahead unchanged. On 12 May 1937, King George VI and Queen

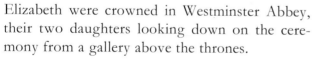

TOP LEFT: *Looking remarkably neatly dressed, the two young princesses dig for victory in the garden at Royal Lodge, Windsor. They and their parents were enthusiastic and hard-working gardeners.*

BELOW LEFT: *Saving petrol in wartime: the Royal Family on bicycles and in a horse and carriage during harvest at Sandringham in 1943.*

BELOW: *Elizabeth's first radio broadcast to the children of Britain and the Empire. Margaret, sitting beside her older sister, joined in to say 'Goodnight, children' at the end of the broadcast.*

RIGHT: *The syringa was in flower at Windsor when this photograph of Princess Elizabeth was taken in 1941.*

Elizabeth were crowned in Westminster Abbey, their two daughters looking down on the ceremony from a gallery above the thrones.

## WARTIME

The shadow of war hung over the first three years of George VI's reign, to be transformed into dreadful reality when Adolf Hitler invaded Poland and Britain declared war on Germany on 3 September 1939. In its early stages there was talk of evacuating the Royal Family to Canada. Queen Elizabeth stopped that. 'The children won't leave without me; I won't leave without the king, and the king will never leave,' she said. The idea was dropped.

The two princesses were kept well away from London, first at Royal Lodge in Windsor Great Park, then in the more heavily fortified Windsor Castle, where for at least a part of the War their sleeping quarters were in a concrete-lined room at the base of one of the castle's ancient towers.

It was from Windsor Castle that Princess Elizabeth made her first radio broadcast, speaking to the children of Britain and the Empire on 'Uncle

Mac's' Children's Hour programme in October 1940. 'I can truthfully say to you all that we children at home are full of cheerfulness and courage,' she said. 'We are trying . . . to bear our share of the danger and sadness of war. We know, everyone of us, that in the end all will be well.'

On the whole the princesses spent the war years in quiet seclusion. Twice, while away from the safety of the castle, they had to take shelter from bombs falling in the Great Park and once Lilibet went to see the wreckage of a German fighter plane which had crashed there. But they were not in the danger that was so close to the king and queen in London, where Buckingham Palace received several direct hits. Both the London houses of Lilibet's earliest years, 17 Bruton Street and 145 Piccadilly, were destroyed, as was Buckingham Palace's private chapel, where she had been christened.

There were numerous photo sessions to provide the world with morale-boosting pictures of the Royal Family doing their bit for the war effort, with the princesses being photographed digging for victory in the garden of Royal Lodge, or helping

with the harvest at Sandringham, and from time to time there were portraits of the heir to the throne, to keep her in the public awareness.

At Windsor, school proceeded much as before and Princess Elizabeth continued her lessons in constitutional history with the Vice-Provost of Eton College, Sir Henry Marten, a delightfully eccentric man not beyond addressing the princess as 'Gentlemen', as if she were a whole classful of Eton boys.

Her father, who once said that he had never been shown a state paper in his life before he became king, was also concerned that the princess should be well grounded in the realities of the great position she would one day be called on to assume, and there were numerous study sessions at the king's desk for the teenage princess. In 1943 the Regency Act was amended so that the king's elder daughter could become a counsellor of state at 18 instead of 21.

Life was far from being all work and no play, however. The princesses' Girl Guides company had been re-formed at Windsor, this time including some London cockney girls, from whom 'Lilibet',

FAR LEFT: *King George VI introducing his daughter to some of the duties of sovereignty. They were photographed at the king's desk at Windsor Castle in 1942.*

BELOW LEFT: *Princess Elizabeth gets her hands dirty while changing a tyre as part of her ATS training.*

LEFT: *VE Day: the Royal Family and the prime minister, Winston Churchill, acknowledge the cheers from the balcony of Buckingham Palace.*

as they casually called her, following the example of her sister Margaret Rose, picked up a passable cockney accent.

There were numerous parties and gatherings of relatives and friends, and every Christmas there was another 'Windsor pantomime', with starring roles for the princesses. At Christmas 1940 a nativity play was put on at Windsor, but after that it was traditional panto, starting with *Cinderella* in 1941, with Margaret as Cinderella and Elizabeth, in satin breeches and braided tunic (vetted for length by her father), as Prince Charming. After that came *Sleeping Beauty*, *Aladdin* and *Old Mother Red Riding Boots*, a merging of several old nursery stories. At each, there were audiences of several hundred, properly printed programmes, and professionally painted scenery and spectacular costumes.

The elder princess was very much alive to her responsibilities in war-time Britain. As soon as she was 16 she went to the Labour Exchange in Windsor to register for the youth service scheme, as all young people were required to do.

Unlike more ordinary citizens, Princess Elizabeth was given an official appointment, her first, on her 16th birthday, when she was made honorary colonel of the Grenadier Guards. It was a particularly appropriate appointment, since a detachment of the Grenadier Guards had been providing a special guard for the princesses at Windsor throughout the War.

### IN UNIFORM—AT LAST

The princess regularly pestered her father to allow her to do 'proper' war work, but he was reluctant to have his daughter exposed to danger. Although she carried out an increasing number of engagements, many of them aimed at bolstering national morale, it was not until 1945 that the princess had her way and donned uniform.

She became 'No. 230873, Second Subaltern Elizabeth Alexandra Mary' in the Auxiliary Territorial Service in April 1945. Soon, she was in and under cars and lorries at No. 1 Mechanical Transport Training Centre, Camberley, learning to strip and service an engine, drive a heavy goods vehicle and read maps efficiently. She would emerge from these sessions dressed in overalls, 'hands and face dirty with oil and grease, and

LEFT: *Despite rationing and post-War austerity, Princess Elizabeth's marriage to Philip Mountbatten was a joyous event, 'a flash of colour on the hard road we have to travel,' said Winston Churchill.*
RIGHT: *Obviously very happy, Elizabeth and Philip posed for photographers at the beginning of their honeymoon at Broadlands. Somewhere in the background was the princess's corgi, Susan, which went with them.*

knowing all about sparking plugs—it was blissful.

It was also satisfactory to be able to wear khaki—her ATS uniform—when she appeared with her parents, Princess Margaret and the prime minister, Winston Churchill, on the balcony of Buckingham Palace on VE day in May. The huge crowd in front of the palace was delirious with joy at the ending of the war in Europe. King George allowed his daughters, accompanied by a group of young officers, to leave the palace and join them, to be swept along with the exuberant throng.

## LOVE AND MARRIAGE

Running like a gold thread through the pattern of Princess Elizabeth's war years was her growing love for her third cousin, Prince Philip of Greece, a fair and handsome young man she met for the first time at the Royal Naval College in Dartmouth in June 1939. She was 13, he was an 18-year-old naval cadet, the son of Prince and Princess Andrew of Greece and, like Elizabeth, a great-great-grandchild of Queen Victoria. His mother had been a Battenburg and her brother (and Philip's uncle) was Lord Louis Mountbatten, later Earl Mountbatten.

The princess did not forget the young man, even though her country was soon at war and Philip (who was to have a very active and often extremely hazardous war) at sea with the Royal Navy. As the war progressed, more and more of his home leaves were spent at Windsor, and before long he and Elizabeth were exchanging letters and photographs.

In 1944, Philip's cousin, King George of Greece, wrote to George VI broaching the subject of marriage between the two. Elizabeth's father would have none of it, considering her far too young to be thinking of marriage—except, of course, that she *was* thinking of it.

There were political problems about a marriage between Elizabeth and Philip. He was a member of the Greek royal family (which was, in fact, Danish by descent), and post-war political difficulties in Greece meant that it could be unhelpful for the royal cause there for Philip to become a naturalized British subject, something he would have to do if he wanted to remain in the Royal Navy, let alone marry a British princess. (The fact that by virtue of the 1701 Act of Settlement he was already a British subject was not realized by anyone at the time.)

By late summer 1946 the young couple had taken matters into their own hands; Philip proposed at Balmoral and Elizabeth accepted. They would

have to wait nearly a year, which included a long separation while the Royal Family made an extended and—for the king, at least—arduous tour of South Africa early in 1947, before their engagement could be acknowledged officially.

Princess Elizabeth celebrated her 21st birthday in South Africa, making a radio broadcast during which she dedicated herself, for her whole life, to the service of the people of the 'great Imperial Commonwealth to which we all belong'.

While she was away, Prince Philip became naturalized. On the suggestion of the British Home Secretary, Chuter Ede, he took as his surname 'Mountbatten', the anglicized form of his mother's maiden name, Battenburg. Thus it was as plain 'Lieutenant Philip Mountbatten RN' that his engagement to 'the dearly beloved daughter' of King George and Queen Elizabeth was finally announced on 10 July 1947. They were both radiant with happiness, Queen Mary noted when they went to visit her that afternoon.

LEFT: *Princess Elizabeth with her baby son, Charles. Twelve temporary typists had to be hired to reply to the huge numbers of letters and presents which poured into Buckingham Palace after his birth.*
BELOW LEFT: *Out and about in Guernsey during Elizabeth and Philip's tour of the Channel Islands in 1949.*
RIGHT: *Family group at the christening of Princess Anne, born at Clarence House on 21 October 1950.*

The wedding day was 20 November 1947, on the morning of which it was announced that the king had created Philip, His Royal Highness The Duke of Edinburgh, Earl of Merioneth and Baron Greenwich, thus sharing him out nicely among Scotland, Wales and England. Among the guests in Westminster Abbey was a large array of European royalty and, in pleasant contrast, the 'ordinary working men and women' who formed the country's Labour Government. The bride promised to 'love, honour and obey' her husband.

They honeymooned at Broadlands, home of 'Uncle Dickie', Earl Mountbatten of Burma and his wife Edwina, and—perhaps because the attentions of press and public at Broadlands got too much for them—at Birkhall, the family home near Balmoral Castle in Scotland.

Elizabeth and Philip's first year of marriage did not take them far from her family. For a time they occupied an apartment in Kensington Palace while waiting for their new home, the once elegant but now badly war-damaged Clarence House to be made ready for them. But the princess was soon pregnant, and the Edinburghs moved back to

Buckingham Palace, where their son was born on 14 November 1948.

The baby was christened Charles Philip Arthur George in the Music Room of Buckingham Palace, once again using Victoria's lace robe and Prince Albert's gold lily-font. Princess Elizabeth's old perambulator was brought out of storage, and the silver-backed brush with which Queen Elizabeth had brushed her daughter's curls was used again in Charles' nursery.

The Duke and Duchess of Edinburgh and their son moved into Clarence House on 4 July 1949— 'Independence Day', said Philip joyfully, with more than one meaning in mind. Just over a year later, their daughter Anne was born.

When they were first married, the Edinburghs looked forward to many happy years of relatively ordinary family life, she doing her share of royal engagements, he pursuing his career in the Royal Navy. While Philip was still based in England, the young couple made a succession of trips all over Britain, 'introducing' the princess's husband to the people of Scotland, Wales and Northern Ireland, as well as England.

From the autumn of 1949, Philip was back on active service in Malta with the First Cruiser Squadron, of which his uncle Earl Mountbatten, also back in the Navy after a high-profile time as India's last viceroy, was Flag Officer. At Christmas, Elizabeth joined her husband. From now, until the summer of 1951, she spent much of her time commuting between Malta and Britain. There she enjoyed the only really 'ordinary' life she was ever to know. She could buy household provisions in local markets, get her hair done in hairdressing salons and generally enjoy a happy informal life in the midst of the naval community.

Things were not so relaxed in Britain. King George had first shown signs of being unwell at Balmoral in the summer of 1948, complaining of severe cramp in his legs. Early the following year he had to undergo surgery, from which he had not recovered by the time of that major event in the royal year, Trooping the Colour.

Princess Elizabeth took the salute for him, for the first time riding sidesaddle to Horse Guards Parade in a feminine version of the uniform of the Grenadier Guards; by 1951 he had to watch the ceremony, at which his daughter once again took the salute on horseback, on the television set in his bedroom at Buckingham Palace. It was announced that he had influenza; in reality, he was suffering from lung cancer.

### THE EDINBURGHS ABROAD

When it became clear that King George and Queen Elizabeth would not be able to carry out a long-projected tour of Australia and New Zealand at the beginning of 1952, it was decided that Elizabeth and Philip should go instead, hard on the heels of a major tour of their own to the Commonwealth's oldest dominion, Canada.

George VI had a second major operation in September, delaying Elizabeth and Philip's departure for Canada, so they broke with precedence by flying there. It was another sign, like George VI's decision that the Home Secretary need not be in attendance at the births of the Princess's children, that the monarchy was changing to keep pace with the post-War world.

It had been hard for George VI to accept the independence of India in 1947 which had deprived him of the much coveted title of 'Emperor', and equally difficult to accept that India's decision to become a republic within the Commonwealth two years later meant that this great country would no longer owe him any allegiance at all as king, but only acknowledge him as titular head of the Commonwealth. It would be for his beloved daughter to make something great and unique of this new role.

She and Philip began the process in Canada. For Philip, now on 'indefinite leave' from the Royal Navy, one pace behind his wife was his official position. In reality, over the 5 weeks and 16,000 miles of the gruelling Canadian tour, he was

continually at her side, supporting her, filling awkward gaps in conversations with strangers, making her laugh.

### ACCESSION

There was a large gathering of members of the Royal Family at Sandringham for Christmas 1951. It was to be the last of King George's reign. At the end of January at London Airport, he waved his daughter and son-in-law off on the first leg of their trip to Australia and New Zealand. They were flying to Kenya, to enjoy a short holiday break at Sagana Royal Lodge, a hunting lodge in the Aberdare Forest Game Reserve, near Nyeri, which had been a wedding gift from the people of Kenya, before setting off from Mombasa to the Antipodes.

By 5 February, the royal party was happily installed at Sagana Lodge. They chose to spend that night in a small resthouse called Treetops, built 30 feet up a giant fig tree, from which the princess would be able to film the wonderful animal life of Kenya at the watering hole below. Some time during that night, while she was there happily watching rhinos and elephants, she became queen. King George VI was found dead in his bed at Sandringham on the morning of 6 February 1952.

# The First Decade

## 1952–1962

ABOVE: *Elizabeth II arrives in England, 7 February 1952.*
OPPOSITE: *The Coronation 1953.*

THE NEW QUEEN WAS BACK in London by 7 February. At London Airport her uncle the Duke of Gloucester, and Earl Mountbatten boarded her aircraft; standing bare-headed on the tarmac in a sad, black-clad line were representatives of her government, including the prime minister, Winston Churchill, future prime minister Anthony Eden, and former Labour prime minister Clement Atlee.

Queen Elizabeth came down the steps of the aircraft alone to meet them, a small figure dressed in black. There were tears on Winston Churchill's cheeks and Anthony Eden would long remember the poignancy of the occasion. It was a few moments before the Queen could trust herself to speak, then she murmured 'This is a very tragic homecoming.'

Awaiting the Queen at Clarence House were a letter from her mother at Sandringham, and—already—a leather box, still marked 'The King', containing government papers requiring the sovereign's attention. Soon, her grandmother, Queen Mary, would arrive to pay homage to the sixth British sovereign she had known, saying 'Her old Granny and subject must be the first to kiss her hand.'

The next day, the Queen made her Declaration of Accession at St James's Palace and signed the Oath. Afterwards a fanfare of trumpets from the

*'I declare before you all that
my whole life, whether it be long or short,
shall be devoted to your service.'*

TOP LEFT: *A huge and enthusiastic crowd fills the floodlit Mall after the Coronation.*

BELOW LEFT: *The Queen and the Duke of Edinburgh, still in uniform, are joined by Prince Charles and Princess Anne on the balcony of Buckingham Palace after the Queen's Birthday Parade, 1953.*

RIGHT: *The great Stanley Matthews receives his winner's medal from the Queen after Blackpool won the F.A. Cup in May 1953.*

FAR RIGHT: *The Queen made her first Christmas broadcast from Sandringham in 1952.*

### WORLD MILESTONES
1952–1962

**October 1952**
State of Emergency declared in Kenya

**March 1953**
Death of Stalin

**May 1953**
Hilary and Tensing reach top of Mount Everest

**November 1956**
Anti-Soviet uprising in Hungary crushed

**October 1957**
Sputnik I launched by Soviet Union

**January 1959**
Revolution in Cuba— Fidel Castro takes power

**March 1959**
US Pioneer IV in orbit around the sun

**April 1961**
Major Yuri Gagarin becomes the first man in space

balcony of St James's Palace proclaimed her officially Queen—while she watched from behind a lace curtain at an upper window.

King George VI lay in state in Westminster Hall in London for three days, during which more than a third of a million people filed past his funeral bier. Then he was interred at Windsor, the Queen scattering a handful of earth from a silver bowl over the coffin and the Lord Chamberlain breaking his staff of office and throwing the pieces into the grave.

Soon the Queen was deep in the business of monarchy, fulfilling a large number of public engagements and dealing with many matters of state, not the least of which was her Coronation, an occasion which figured in her first Christmas broadcast, made from Sandringham. 'Pray for me on that day,' she said. 'Pray that God may give me the wisdom and strength to carry out the solemn promise I shall be making.' The day chosen for the Coronation was 2 June 1953.

Prominent among the many engagements of her first months as Queen were ones that would recur year after year: her first distribution of the Royal Maundy, during which she gave specially minted silver coins to as many old men and women as the years of her age; her first State Opening of Parliament, which she attended wearing a purple robe and diadem handed down from Queen Victoria; and her first Birthday Parade and Trooping the Colour as Queen. There were many other engagements of a less ceremonious kind; she was even on hand to present the F.A. Cup to Blackpool in 1953.

Queen Mary's death a few weeks before the Coronation brought private grief to the Royal Family but, on the old queen's own instructions, no diminution of the Coronation celebrations.

Although the Coronation was televised—a decision taken by the Queen in the face of opposition from older courtiers—being there was what mattered to hundreds of thousands of her subjects. They came from all over the world, filling every hotel room, including some on ships moored on the Thames, in the capital, and sleeping out along the processional route.

The Coronation and the Queen at the heart of it, became the focus for fervent mass rejoicing on a scale never experienced before—or since. It was as if a new age had dawned, an age signalled by the bells which rang out from Westminster Abbey and the guns which boomed across London at the sacred moment of the Crowning.

## QUEEN AND COMMONWEALTH

The richly bejewelled and embroidered gown worn by the Queen at her Coronation carried the floral emblems of the countries of the Commonwealth alongside the rose, thistle, leek and shamrock of the United Kingdom, thus emphasizing the Queen's role as Head of the Commonwealth, and it was to the Commonwealth that the Queen and her husband went on a major royal tour at the end of Coronation year.

They left England on 24 November 1953 and would be away nearly six months. They travelled nearly 45,000 miles by land, sea and air and, apart from a refuelling stop in Canada, had engagements in Bermuda, Jamaica, Panama, Fiji, Tonga, New Zealand, Australia, the Cocos Islands, Ceylon, Aden, Uganda, Libya, Malta and Gibraltar.

In seven of these countries, the Queen opened sessions of their parliaments, wearing at each her Coronation gown. In hot climates the dress, which weighed 30 lbs (13.5 kg), could be a penance: in Colombo the metal paillettes in the embroidery became too hot to touch. But the Queen considered it essential the gown should be worn—it was a symbolic part of the practical exercise in bonding the countries of the Commonwealth which she was engaged upon on this tour.

She was also emphasizing her own place at the head of the Commonwealth. In her Christmas broadcast for 1953, made from Auckland, New Zealand, she outlined one purpose of her tour: 'I want to show that the Crown is not merely an abstract symbol of our unity but a personal and living bond between you and me,' she told her listeners in every country of the Commonwealth. Later, when opening the Australian parliament in February 1954, she spelled out her position. 'It is my resolve that under God I shall not only rule but serve. This describes, I believe, the modern character of the British Crown.'

Apart from these great state occasions, much of the tour was taken up with meeting people and getting to know the countries the Queen was visiting for the first time. It has been estimated that the Queen and the Duke of Edinburgh attended 223 balls, receptions, sports meetings and garden parties; the Queen made 157 speeches (Queen Mary once confessed that she had only ever made two speeches in her whole life) and the Duke of Edinburgh made a good few on his own account; and that she shook up to 13,000 hands.

In Tonga, the Queen met a descendant of Fletcher Christian, the *Bounty* mutineer, and a giant turtle called Tuimalila, 'King of the Palace', who had been alive in the time of Fletcher Christian himself and of Captain Cook. In New Zealand and Australia, the Queen got to know all about sheep-shearing and timber felling, and went to the races—where she had the rather uncanny experience of having all the race-goers' glasses trained on her rather than the horses. In Adelaide, half a million people lined the streets to see her, while she heard several of the 162 renditions of 'God Save the Queen' which were to come her way during her 57 days in Australia.

Much of the royal tour's travelling between one country and the next was done on board a gleaming white Shaw Savill company liner, *Gothic*, and it was not until Tobruk was reached that the Queen was able to board her new yacht, *Britannia*. On board, to her great joy, were her children who, for the previous six months, she had known only as voices on the telephone.

The Queen's homecoming, sailing up the Channel in early May, 1954, was an occasion for almost as much joyful celebration as the Coronation had been, and an armada of small boats came out to escort the Royal Family home.

On board *Britannia* was the British prime minister, Winston Churchill, who had joined the yacht off The Needles. Six months before, he had sent his sovereign off with the ringing words 'It may well be that the journey the Queen is about to take will be no less auspicious, and the treasures she brings back no less bright, than when Drake first sailed an English ship around the world.' The journey remains the longest single tour undertaken in a reign remarkable for the amount of travelling the sovereign has done.

Once back in Britain, the Queen very quickly returned to the routine of royal life which she had inherited from her father and grandfather. Thus, the spring and summer of 1954 saw a succession of public engagements in various parts of the country, and late summer brought the Royal Family to Balmoral, where the increasingly ailing Winston Churchill travelled to stay with the Queen—another tradition of royal life which the prime minister insisted on respecting.

In fact, Churchill, who had suffered several small strokes, was clearly reaching the end of his parliamentary career and would soon have to make way for a younger, fitter man. Before this, however, there was another State Opening of Parliament to precede the autumn session, and his 80th Birthday to be celebrated in fitting style at the end of November.

It was not until early 1955 that Churchill finally made up his mind to resign, and the manner of his going would be as much on the grand scale as anything else in his colourful career: he would be the first prime minister to invite his sovereign to a farewell dinner at 10 Downing Street, the official residence of Britain's prime ministers. The famous dinner took place on 4 April 1955 and the next day Churchill resigned. Anthony Eden, whom the Queen had made a Knight of the Garter some months before, became prime minister.

While Churchill's resignation caused the Queen to give more than a little thought to the royal prerogative and her exercising of it—no doubt asking herself what she could have done if Churchill had clearly become too incapacitated to carry on, or whether she could take an outgoing prime minister's advice on who his successor could be—another constitutional question was blowing up into a storm much nearer home.

TOP: *The Queen drives to the State Opening of Parliament, November 1954.*

ABOVE: *Prime minister Winston Churchill says farewell to the Queen after the dinner party at Downing Street which preceded his resignation in 1955. Lady Churchill is in the background.*

TOP RIGHT: *Undaunted by the rain, children wave happily to the Queen during her visit to Truro in Cornwall, in May 1956.*

## PRINCESS MARGARET'S DILEMMA

At the centre of this trouble was Princess Margaret and her desire to marry a divorced man, Group Captain Peter Townsend.

Townsend had been the innocent party in his divorce but the Church of England did not countenance divorce at all and the Queen, as head of the established Church of England, could not countenance it either. In 1953 the Queen had been advised by her prime minister that such a marriage would be disastrous for the Crown, and Margaret and her Group Captain had parted for two years.

Now, the princess was close to her 25th birthday, when she would no longer need the Queen's consent to her marriage. Under the terms of the Royal Marriages Act, passed in 1772 to keep George III's unsatisfactory sons in some sort of marital order, the princess would have to give the Queen and Parliament a year's notice of her intention to marry. Parliament could choose to refuse her a grant from the Civil List, and she might be required to retire into private life, and certainly she could have only a civil marriage, unblessed by the Church—but she could marry.

The storm which blew about the beleaguered princess and her deeply distressed sister proved too strong. Towards the end of October 1955, Anthony Eden told the Queen that his government could not support the princess in her wish to marry, and *The Times* newspaper came out with an editorial totally against the princess. She and Townsend gave up. In a statement which he helped her to write, the princess said 'Mindful of the Church's teaching that Christian marriage is indissoluble, and conscious of my duty to the Commonwealth, I have resolved to put these considerations before any other.'

## SUEZ AND AFTER

1956 saw the beginning of the end of Elizabeth II's honeymoon period as sovereign. That this should coincide with the great Suez debacle, which dented British pride and the country's standing in the world, was no accident; the Queen, as the moral head of the nation, must perforce be closely linked with its image, both in the eyes of the country's people and in those of outsiders.

Even Marilyn Monroe, in Britain that summer to film *The Prince and The Showgirl* with Lawrence Olivier, remarked at one of her press conferences that Britain seemed to have a lot on its mind—and she meant more than just her gorgeous self.

When, in the middle of the political storm caused by the Suez invasion, Eden fell ill and went to the West Indies to recuperate, he left R.A. Butler, who had not been wholeheartedly behind the Suez adventure, deputizing for him in the Cabinet. Although Eden returned apparently fit and well before the end of 1956, he was ill again by the New Year, and resigned on 9 January 1957.

Conservatives outside the parliamentary party assumed that Rab Butler would get Eden's job, and Butler's claim was heavily backed by the press. So it came as a surprise to many when the Queen, apparently acting just on the advice of Lord Salisbury, the President of the Council, invited Harold Macmillan, the Chancellor of the Exchequer, to form a government. In fact, Lord Salisbury had been little more than a messenger conveying the preference of the Conservative Party in Parliament for Harold rather than Rab. But the impression had been given that the Queen had allowed herself to be influenced by the 'tweedy' land-owning people who dominated her private world.

During 1957, the Queen and Prince Philip made four state visits, to Portugal, France, Denmark and the United States and Canada. It was while the royal couple were in America that a controversy that had already raged for some weeks in Britain

ABOVE LEFT: *The Queen meets the Queen of Hollywood, Marilyn Monroe, at the Royal Command Film Performance in London, October 1956. To Marilyn's right is the film star, Victor Mature. The film they all saw was a wartime drama,* The Battle of the River Plate.

RIGHT: *The Queen in Paris during her state visit to France in 1957, a year in which she and the Duke of Edinburgh made three other European visits.*

was given a new lease of life in an American magazine, *The Saturday Evening Post*.

In Britain, a young peer had published an article in which he attacked with vim and vigour the Queen's court. They were 'almost without exception the "tweedy" sort' wrote Lord Altrincham, and had failed to live with the times. The words they put into the Queen's mouth 'made her sound like a priggish schoolgirl' . . . and so on. *The Saturday Evening Post*'s piece, by the British writer Malcolm Muggeridge, was titled 'Does Britain Really Need a Queen', which was something of a misrepresentation of Muggeridge's views, but which got the controversy going nicely again.

Most older British people were, like the Queen, outraged; but the *Daily Mail* newspaper conducted a poll of their readers which showed that a majority of younger ones thought that the two writers had a few valid points. Prince Philip thought so, too.

Eventually, the fuss died down, though there were perhaps some lessons learned at the Palace and one or two points in the Altrincham/Muggeridge case noted. Indeed, the Queen had been making moves to widen the Palace's horizons even before her critics had opened fire on her.

In 1956, for instance, she had begun giving informal luncheon parties to which people prominent in everyday life—businessmen, sports people, industrialists, people active in the arts or working

in the National Health Service—were invited to meet her and one or two other members of her family. She had already decided, too, that after 1958 there would be no more of those tedious debutante presentations at which girls from 'good' or moneyed families filed past her in long lines as part of their introduction into 'society'.

A major move towards opening up the rather closed world of parliament to outside talent and experience, came with the creation of life peerages. This was a scheme of Harold Macmillan, and one of which the Queen greatly approved. She announced it in the Speech from the Throne during the State Opening of Parliament in November 1957 and the first life barons and baronesses were announced the following July, the same month in which the Queen announced, at the close of the Commonwealth Games in Cardiff, that she intended creating her son Charles Prince of Wales.

Christmas 1957 saw the first Royal Broadcast to be televised. Since videotape was not yet available, the Queen had to scramble through her Christmas lunch to make the broadcast live from the Library at Sandringham.

Watching the broadcast at Sandringham was Prince Charles, home from school for the holidays:

BOTTOM LEFT: *The Queen looks slim and dashing in miner's overalls and helmet as she prepares to go on an underground visit at the Rothes Colliery in Kirkcaldy, Fife, in 1958.*
TOP LEFT: *The Queen and the Duke with President and Mrs John F. Kennedy at a dinner held in honour of America's leader, at Buckingham Palace in June 1961.*
RIGHT: *The Service of Remembrance at the Cenotaph in London, November 1960. The Queen attends the ceremony each year.*

perhaps the greatest change in her family's way of life made by the Queen in 1957 was to send her son to boarding school. In this she was no doubt influenced by the Duke of Edinburgh who had had most of his education at British boarding schools. Cheam, where Charles was now a boarder, had been Philip's first school in England.

Eventually, all the Queen's children were given boarding school educations, two of her sons going on to university to achieve very respectable degrees. At this stage, of course, her two younger sons had not yet been born, since the Queen's early accession to the throne had meant her putting aside all thoughts of increasing her family. It was while on a trip to Canada in June 1959, during which the Queen and President Dwight Eisenhower jointly opened the new St Lawrence Seaway, that the Queen revealed that she was pregnant again. She refused to curtail the trip, and her second son, Prince Andrew Albert Christian Edward, was safely born in February 1960.

Within weeks of her son's birth, the Queen was welcoming the President of France, General de Gaulle, on a state visit to Britain, and not long after that she was happily attending the wedding of her sister Margaret to Mr Anthony Armstrong-Jones in Westminster Abbey.

### THE CHANGING COMMONWEALTH

In February 1960, Harold Macmillan on a trip to Africa, made his famous 'wind of change' speech in the Parliament of South Africa. In fact, in all parts of the Commonwealth, change was to the fore as once dependent colonies and outposts of Empire grew to independence. Ghana had chosen to become a republic in 1958 and Cyprus would do the same later in 1960.

It was as Head of the Commonwealth that the Queen visited India and Pakistan, as well as Nepal and Iran, early in 1961. The trip was a very successful one, though Prince Philip had to develop a diplomatic whitlow on a finger to avoid a tiger hunt in Nepal, so great had been the outcry back in Britain over the tiger that he had taken part in hunting and killing during his trip to India.

At this time, the Queen and her staff were making plans for a trip to north-west Africa late in 1961 knowing that at the other end of the great continent, Macmillan's wind of change was blow-ing up into a hurricane over the question of apartheid. The Commonwealth Prime Ministers' Conference in 1960 had achieved no solution to this major problem, despite the best diplomatic efforts of those present, including the Queen.

In May 1961, the white citizens of South Africa voted to become a republic and to leave the Commonwealth. It was a particularly sad blow for the Queen, who had made her vow of life-long service to the Commonwealth in Cape Town.

It was a low point in an otherwise lively year. Dressed in black lace and diamonds, the Queen visited Pope John XXIII in the Vatican with her husband and shortly after welcomed into her own home America's first Roman Catholic President, John F. Kennedy and his glamorous wife. America had recently voted the Queen the 'Third Most

LEFT AND BOTTOM RIGHT: *Contrasting modes of transport during the royal tour of India and Pakistan in 1961. A richly caparisoned elephant carries the Queen in Benares, India, and a white Cadillac is used for a drive through the streets of Karachi, Pakistan.*

TOP RIGHT: *The Queen wears a favourite tiara, Queen Mary's 'fringe' tiara, in 1962. The older Queen left her personal fortune to the reigning sovereign on her death in 1953.*

Admired Woman in the World', after Eleanor Roosevelt and Jacqueline Kennedy. The Queen probably took this vote with a pinch of salt, just as she would the later poll in a British national newspaper which revealed that Prince Philip was thought to be potentially 'Britain's best dictator', in the event of the country's needing such a thing.

The year ended with an enormously successful tour of Ghana, Liberia and Sierra Leone, which the Queen and her husband undertook in the face of the grave misgivings of the British Government, so volatile did the political situation look in Kwame Nkrumah's Ghana. The Queen and Prince Philip were welcomed with excitement and joy wherever they went, however, and the Queen herself, betraying no fear or alarm at the troubles in the background, was never in any real danger.

# The Commonwealth

The Commonwealth is an entirely voluntary organization—a free association of 50 sovereign independent states, with a total population of more than 1,394,600,000 people – about a quarter of the world's total. The historical fact that links them all is that they were formerly part of the British Empire.

The Commonwealth has its origins way back in the famous Durham Report of 1839, though of more recent significance was an Imperial Conference in 1926, the principles arising from which were given legal substance by the 1932 Statute of Westminster.

A major change of direction came in George VI's reign when the newly independent India decided in 1949 to become a republic, but to remain in the Commonwealth. The other members of the Commonwealth agreed that India could remain within the group, accepting the King as 'the symbol of the free association of its independent member nations and as such the Head of the Commonwealth'. At the time of the Queen's accession, members of the Commonwealth agreed to recognize her as the new Head of the Commonwealth, a position not vested in the British crown.

Today's Commonwealth is a much larger organization than George VI knew, and his daughter is now Head of a Commonwealth that includes 27 republics, four monarchies (Lesotho, Brunei, Swa-

LEFT: *The Queen, wearing her Coronation gown, opens the New Zealand Parliament during her Commonwealth tour of 1953–54.*
BELOW RIGHT: *The Queen with Scouts from the Commonwealth at the* Scouts' annual St George's Day Parade, Windsor, April 1967.
ABOVE: *Commonwealth heads of government photographed with the Queen at St James's Palace during the 1966 Commonwealth Conference.*

ziland and Tonga), one country with a Paramount Chief (Western Samoa) and one, Malaysia, where the Head of State is elected for five years from among nine hereditary rulers. This still leaves 17 nations of which the queen is the Head of State. These countries are Antigua and Barbuda, Australia, the Bahamas, Barbados, Belize, Britain, Canada, Grenada, Jamaica, Mauritius, New Zealand, Papua New Guinea, St Christopher and Nevis, Saint Vincent and the Grenadines, Solomon

Islands and Tuvalu. In these countries, except Britain, the Queen is personally represented by a Governor General, whom she appoints on the advice of the government of the country concerned.

The Queen's connections with the Commonwealth have always been close. She was in South Africa when she made the famous speech dedicating her life to the service of the 'great Imperial Commonwealth to which we all belong', and she was in Kenya when the death of her father made her Queen. Today, South Africa is no longer a part of the Commonwealth, having been the first country in her reign to sever all connections with it (in 1961); and Kenya chose to become a republic within the Commonwealth in 1964, the year after it became an independent nation. Fiji left the Commonwealth in 1987, while Pakistan, which had

severed its links with the Commonwealth in 1972, was brought back into the fold by Benazir Bhutto in 1989.

The Commonwealth Heads of Government regularly hold meetings and conferences. During the early years of her reign, the Queen only attended those held in Britain. But the 1973 conference was to be held in Ottawa, and the Canadian prime minister, Pierre Trudeau, invited the Queen to attend. That conference was a great success. It was also a very different affair from the first such conference of the Queen's reign, when Winston Churchill chaired a conference in London of the heads of government of only eight countries.

Since 1973, the Queen has managed to attend most Commonwealth Conferences, wherever they are held. Occasionally—notably at Lusaka in 1979—there have been doubts about the Queen's attending, but her presence has always been judged invaluable. Again, that 1979 conference is often cited as an example of the way in which the Queen's soothingly diplomatic presence in the background can contribute a great deal towards a successful and harmonious outcome.

Most Commonwealth leaders agree that the Queen gives the Commonwealth continuity; prime ministers and heads of government come and go; but the Queen remains a constant and very well-

ABOVE LEFT: *With the President of India, Dr Radkakrishnan, at the Commonwealth Institute in London, June 1963.*
LEFT: *The Queen with all the Commonwealth heads of government at Buckingham Palace in 1977. These formal photographs are becoming a feature of the annual Conferences—the numbers attending have risen dramatically since the early days, and have increased even more since this photograph was taken.*

ABOVE RIGHT: *The Queen and the Duke of Edinburgh with the Indian prime minister, Mrs Indira Gandhi, at Rashtrapata Bhavan during the royal tour of India in 1983. Mrs. Gandhi was assassinated shortly afterwards.*

informed figure. She makes sure that at every conference she has a private talk with each head of government there, giving each one the same amount of time, and showing the same detailed knowledge of and interest in each member country.

The Queen sees herself—or, more correctly, the Crown—as 'a human link between all people who owe allegiance to me—an allegiance of mutual love and respect and never of compulsion'. She also agrees with other Commonwealth leaders that there are other less tangible but important links. As President Kaunda of Zambia said in London in 1977, 'Today, we have an organization not serving the British people and the British communities abroad but mankind as a whole. We are not members of this Commonwealth by accident of colonial history but by conviction.'

*Two-year-old Anne with her doll's pram.*

# Family Album
## 1952 – 1962

The early years of Elizabeth II's reign involved adjusting to a very different way of life for everyone. For herself, although duty came first, there were some changes she could make to her father's routine so that her children, at least, did not lose out. Her prime minister was asked to come to his weekly audience at Buckingham Palace 30 minutes later so that the Queen could have the precious tea and bath-before-bed hour with Charles and Anne.

For the Queen's husband, things were very difficult at first. There was now no question of his returning to the Royal Navy, but there seemed no real role for him out of it, not even as head of his household, as he had been

*Charles's toy car is a perfectly scaled model.*

in Clarence House. Perhaps his worst moment came when the Queen, on the advice of her prime minister and private secretary, announced two months after her Accession that she and her children would be known as the House and Family of Windsor, thus setting aside her husband's name, Mountbatten. Some consolation came just before the birth of Prince Andrew, when another Order in Council changed the surname of younger members of the Royal Family to Mountbatten-Windsor.

The Queen's mother, too, had changed her title, announcing that she wished to be known as Queen Elizabeth the Queen Mother, rather than the more usual Dowager Queen Elizabeth. Within her family she is always known as 'Queen Elizabeth', with her daughter being referred to simply as 'The Queen'.

At Easter 1952, the young Royal Family's possessions were moved along the Mall to Buckingham Palace and Queen Elizabeth and her daughter Margaret moved into Clarence House.

FAMILY MILESTONES
1952–1962
**March 1953**
Death of Queen Mary
**February 1960**
Birth of Prince Andrew
**February 1960**
Death of Edwina, Countess Mountbatten of Burma
**May 1960**
Marriage of Princess Margaret to
Anthony Armstrong-Jones (later Earl of Snowdon)
**June 1961**
Marriage of Edward, Duke of Kent to
Miss Katherine Worsley
**November 1961**
Birth of David Viscount Linley, son of
Princess Margaret and Lord Snowdon

*With the children at Balmoral, 1952.*

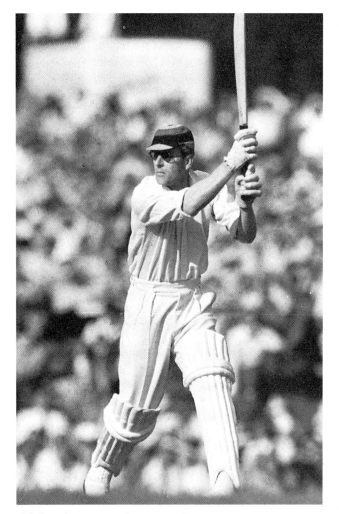

*Philip playing in a charity match, 1953.*

From the earliest days of her reign, family life for the Queen was at its most complete outside London, in her country homes in three quite distinct parts of the United Kingdom.

Balmoral, on the Dee in what is now the Grampian region of Scotland, was built by Victoria and Albert as their much loved Highland home, and remains essential to the Queen's comfort. There she and Philip took their children in the first summer of her reign, to enjoy real peace and privacy. House parties were friendly and relaxed and the entertainment was very much centred on the outdoors.

Sandringham, near King's Lynn in Norfolk,

*Helping at Mummy's sale of work in aid of the Crathie Church Vestry, 1955.*

*An improvised seesaw at Balmoral. Whisky looks amused!*

was bought as his country house by Victoria's son, later Edward VII. Here, too, the new Queen and her family continued the established country house way of life, though the Duke of Edinburgh soon sent the breeze of modern business practice through the Sandringham farms, aiming to make them more commercially profitable.

For the Queen, a particular joy at Sandringham was the stable and stud at which, from the outset of her reign, she followed her greatest personal interest, the breeding of racehorses. She had hoped to have a Derby winner in her Coronation year, but her horse Aureole was beaten and would not come triumphantly good for two more years.

Royal Windsor, in Berkshire, was and remains the Royal Family's regular weekend home. One of the Queen's first Christmas presents to her new husband had been a polo pony and he pursued this exciting sport with great enthusiasm, mainly at Windsor. It was at Smith's Lawn, in Windsor Great Park, that many of the young Royal Family's early summer Sunday afternoons were spent, watching Philip playing polo.

*The Queen after her first Christmas speech on TV, 1957.*

*Watching polo at Smith's Lawn, Windsor, in 1958.*

*This photograph was taken on the East Terrace Garden steps at Windsor Castle in June 1959.*

*Margaret's wedding day; Philip gave the bride away.*

*At the Oaks, 1960. Aunt Mary studies her race card.*

By the end of the first decade of the Queen's reign, her private life had settled into a pleasant routine. The immediate circle of the Royal Family had grown with the birth of Prince Andrew and of Princess Margaret's first child, David, Viscount Linley, but it was still not so large that everyone could not fit happily into Sandringham for Christmas. The Queen still made the journey by train, as she had done since her childhood, and photographs of the departure were regular features in newspapers at Christmastime.

Also regularly photographed were annual visits to Epsom racecourse for the Derby and the Oaks, the race for fillies which the Queen's horse Carrozza, ridden by Lester Piggott, won in 1957.

*Leaving Sandringham with Andrew, Christmas 1961.*

# The
# Second Decade
## 1962–1972

ABOVE: *The Queen on her throne in the House of Lords, 1967.* RIGHT: *The Investiture of the Prince of Wales, 1969*

ELIZABETH II'S SECOND decade as sovereign coincided with a period of great change in social attitudes throughout the Western World. The 1960s became the decade of the Beatles and the mini-skirt, of Flower Power and the beginnings of feminism.

It was also a decade of heightened political tension, punctuated by the violent deaths of world leaders—John F. Kennedy in the United States in 1963, the South African prime minister Dr Verwoerd in 1966, and Martin Luther King and Robert Kennedy in 1968—and clouded by war and revolt, from Vietnam and the Middle East to the Congo and Czechoslovakia, from students in Paris to extremists in the United Kingdom. Even the Investiture of the Queen's eldest son as Prince of Wales in 1969 was over-shadowed by the very real threat of violence from Welsh Nationalist extremists.

Just as the Queen showed no sign of fear or apprehension during the Investiture at Caernarvon Castle, so she gave no hint as to her opinion of all these manifestations of a changing world and changing values. True, she smiled broadly when she met the Beatles and, unlike some of her more crusty subjects, apparently made no objection to their being awarded MBEs. Unlike her daughter Anne, she never wore a mini-skirt, the lower half of the royal knee being as much as she ever showed, and we do not know if *The*

'. . .*I still can't believe he is really mine . . .*'

50

*Female Eunuch*, an early feminist book published in 1970, ever found its way on to the Queen's reading list, even if it was written by an Australian subject, Germaine Greer.

Indeed, the Queen seemed intent on showing herself to be moderate in all things—a sensible, family-orientated young woman and mother of four children (her youngest child, Edward, being born in 1964), to whom the old ways were, if not necessarily the best, still as good as anything the 'modern' world could show. Not that new ways were ignored in Buckingham Palace. Far from it.

While the Queen, her mother and sister continued their active support of excellent and long-established organizations such as the Boy Scout and Girl Guide movements, Prince Philip approached the welfare of Britain's young people from new, very practical angles. He gave his active support to the Duke of Edinburgh Awards Scheme, which opened up new opportunities for children from all social backgrounds, and his patronage to the National Playing Fields Association.

In other ways, the Queen continued into the 1960s the early determination shown by her and her

LEFT: *The Queen at the 1962 'Gang Show', the variety show put on by the Boy Scouts and Girl Guides, held at the Golders Green Empire, London.*
RIGHT: *On her Australian tour in 1963, the Queen talked to users of the Flying Doctor Service's radio network.*
FAR RIGHT: *A Buckingham Palace Garden Party, July 1964. By the mid-1960s, the garden parties, with which the Queen replaced the 'coming out' balls for debutantes, had become major events. Thousands of guests from all walks of life could enjoy the Palace's 40 acres of gardens and, perhaps, meet a member of the Royal Family, before taking tea or iced coffee at one of the tea tents.*

husband to make the monarchy more accessible to more of her subjects. The Royal Garden Parties—three a year at Buckingham Palace and one at the Palace of Holyroodhouse in Edinburgh—were now established as regular events in the royal calendar, each one giving some 7,000 people the opportunity to visit the Queen and her family at home, taking tea in her exquisite gardens while military bands played selections of popular tunes.

The opening in 1962 of the Queen's Gallery in Buckingham Palace, on the site of the bombed royal chapel, allowed the Queen's subjects to become acquainted with the riches of the royal collections. Now, priceless treasures from the royal collections of art, furniture and even stamps, could be enjoyed by the public. The first exhibition, called 'Treasures from the Royal Collection', attracted more than 200,000 people and the second, 'Royal Children', enabled everyone to note resemblances between some members of the present Royal Family and the children of King George III, as depicted in the magnificent paintings of Thomas Gainsborough.

## SEEING THE WORLD

Firmly ignoring George V's remark that 'Abroad is awful—I know because I've been there', the Queen and Prince Philip continued to go overseas a great deal. Having already notched up several records for royal travel, including the first circumnavigation of the globe by a reigning monarch and the longest tour to be undertaken by British royalty, the Queen continued into the 1960s the series of state visits and Commonwealth tours begun at the outset of her reign. Not that she regarded visits to Commonwealth countries, such as Australia and New Zealand where she and Prince Philip went in 1963, as going 'abroad'; rather, these countries of which she was Queen were seen as an extension of 'home'. All too aware that they were parts of 'home' where she 'had to be seen to be believed', she tried to make her visits regular and not too far apart. Sending all her sons to schools in the Commonwealth in the 1960s and '70s—Charles to Australia, Andrew to Canada and Edward to New Zealand—was part of the process of forging close ties with these 'homes' abroad.

Of course, not all the newly independent countries of the Commonwealth recognized Elizabeth II as their queen. The early 1960s saw independence come to a great many former colonies and dependent territories and many, including Nigeria, Zambia and Kenya, chose to become republics within the Commonwealth, recognizing the Queen as Head of that great family of nations.

The Queen's first direct brush with that stream of violent protest which would be one of the themes of the 1960s came in 1964 in Canada, the oldest dominion of the Commonwealth. 'Liz Go Home!' said the banners brandished at her in Quebec, where separatists refused to acknowledge that, as Queen of Canada, she *was* at home.

There were threats of an assassination which, it was said, would turn Quebec, less than a year after John F. Kennedy's murder, into a second Dallas. The Queen ignored them, carrying out all her engagements in the city, albeit from the shelter of a bullet-proof car and surrounded by police marksmen.

If she was relieved to return to the United Kingdom, where she now had for the first time in her reign a Labour-led government, she was careful not to show it. Just as she was careful not to show her distaste for the over-enthusiastic greeting she received in Berlin while on a state visit to West Germany a few months later: the almost ritualistic chanting of her name seemed a bit too much of a good thing, and the Queen took more pleasure in the quieter moments of her visit, including meetings with her husband's family.

## CHANGING ROLES

If West Germany was demonstrating a brilliant ability to put the past behind it and become a leading member of the new Europe, Britain, too, was a different country from the one which had survived the Second World War. Elizabeth II was reigning over a very different society from the one her father and grandfather had known.

The death of Winston Churchill early in 1965 and the magnificent pageantry of his state funeral, firmly marked the end of an era which had already passed into history with the end of Harold Macmillan's premiership in 1963 and the victory of Harold Wilson's Labour Party over the Conservatives and Sir Alec Douglas-Home in October 1964. The Queen had been drawn into the choice of Sir Alec as Macmillan's successor, but the Labour Party's leader had been chosen by the party itself and in the years ahead Britain's other political parties would also adopt carefully regulated ways of choosing their leaders, leaving the sovereign with no real part to play in the proceedings.

If the Queen's political role seemed less significant, her role as head of state, as someone to give the country a moral lead, seemed to grow in

LEFT: *The Queen meets the residents of Queensferry House for Old People, Edinburgh, in July 1965.*
FAR LEFT: *As Sovereign of the Order of the Bath, an order with both civilian and military knights, the Queen attends a service for the* Order *in Westminster Abbey, 1964.*
BELOW: *Earl Mountbatten of Burma in full ceremonial uniform as Governor of the Isle of Wight greets the Queen at Carisbrooke Castle on the island in July 1965.*

stature. Her public engagements took her the length and breadth of the land, linking people at one end of the country with those in the other—the residents of an old people's home in Edinburgh, say, with the people of the Isle of Wight. As for the country as a whole, who better to express the national will, as she had done earlier in 1965 when she inaugurated the British memorial to President John F. Kennedy at Runnymede.

### UDI AND AFTER

On one level the Queen's life in the second half of the 1960s moved with apparently unchanging serenity through its familiar annual round: New Year at Sandringham, Easter at Windsor, summer at Balmoral, Christmas at Windsor, always held 'firm in the web of family relationships—between parents and children, grandparents and grandchildren, aunts and uncles', as the Queen would herself describe family life during the celebrations of her Silver Wedding anniversary in 1972.

The Queen's public life, on the other hand, seemed extraordinarily busy, with her engagements diary and its newspaper summary, the Court Circular (still written in terms similar to those used in Queen Victoria's day), indicating the points of change and of stability in the world of the mid-twentieth century. Emphasizing the historical continuity of life, the diary could point to the Queen's participation in the celebrations of the 700th anniversary of Parliament and the 900th anniversary of Westminster Abbey, both in 1965. Showing history coming to terms with the modern age, the diary would note that the State Opening of Parliament after the 1966 General Election (winner, Mr Harold Wilson's Labour Party) was the first one to be televised, while an engagement at the British Aircraft Corporation's works at Filton near Bristol was pure twentieth century, for the Queen went there to check up on progress in the exciting—and expensive—Anglo-French project to build a supersonic aircraft, to be called Concorde.

Foremost among the Queen's concerns outside the United Kingdom at this time was the question of Southern Rhodesia, where the white minority wanted independence without black majority rule. Rhodesian prime minister Ian Smith's unilateral declaration of independence in November 1965 was a rejection both of Britain's right to have any say in the affairs of Rhodesia and of any idea of loyalty towards the Queen and her Crown.

While the Rhodesia question would hang heavily over British and Commonwealth affairs for years to come, it did not curb the Queen's travels outside Britain. Many of the nearly fifty countries

LEFT: *The Queen opens the Commonwealth Building of the Post-Graduate Medical School at Hammersmith, west London, in 1966.*
ABOVE: *Taking a keen interest in the shape of things to come, the Queen studies a model of Concorde in September 1966, two-and-a-half years before the British Concorde's maiden flight. The Queen was visiting the British Aircraft Corporation's works at Filton, near Bristol.*

the Queen and Prince Philip visited during the decade were Commonwealth ones, and its importance was confirmed in 1966 with the decision that 11 June (the Queen's official birthday that year) would be observed as Commonwealth Day. The following month, Malawi, Rhodesia's neighbour, became a republic within the Commonwealth.

For most people in Britain, however, 1966 was a year to figure in everyone's lives for events in no way connected with the Commonwealth. In July, England won the World Cup and the Queen was there to see football's greatest trophy won in triumph. Three months later, triumph had become tragedy in the Welsh mining village of Aberfan, where 144 people, 116 of them children in school, were killed when a mining tip buried one end of the village. The Queen's face when she went to Aberfan, expressed the grief of the whole nation.

### FOUNT OF HONOUR

The Queen is formally the source of all honours and distinctions, a legacy from medieval times when the king personally rewarded deserving followers with grants of land, money, jewels and titles. Today, of course, the machinery that keeps the honours system flourishing is government-run. Even so, it is the Queen who is perceived to be bestowing the honours, most often at the investitures she holds at Buckingham Palace several times a year.

Sometimes an honour is bestowed at a private ceremony, such as the time the Queen knighted the captain of the *Gothic* on board his ship at the end of her great world tour in 1953–4. Sometimes an award is deemed so special that its presentation is a major event. The knighting of Francis Chichester at Greenwich on 7 July 1967 was such an occasion, the choice of the historic palace with its rich

maritime connections giving added romance and colour to the event, which was held outdoors near the Thames, so that many people could join in the celebrations in honour of the heroic yachtsman.

There are more than thirty different kinds of award—ribbons, badges, stars and titles—which may be awarded to Britons (and to the citizens of those Commonwealth countries which have chosen to remain within the British honours system). In each of the two main honours lists issued every year—the New Year's honours list and the Queen's Birthday honours list announced on the Queen's official birthday in June—the number of awards averages more than 2,000.

Of all the awards and honours, the most highly valued and the most distinguished is also the most simple: the Order of Merit confers no titles or grand robes, just a badge which may be worn around the neck on a ribbon by the twenty-four

LEFT: *Francis Chichester sailed single-handed round the world in his small boat,* Gipsy Moth IV *in 1966–7. The Queen used Sir Francis Drake's sword to knight Chichester in a historic open-air ceremony held at Greenwich in July 1967.*

RIGHT: *The Queen visiting Christ Church, one of Oxford University's many distinguished colleges, in May 1968.*

men and women of distinction who may hold it at any one time. The Order of Merit is one of four awards that the Queen makes herself, without having to submit them formally to the prime minister of the day. The others are the Most Noble Order of the Garter, the Most Ancient and Most Noble Order of the Thistle and the Royal Victorian Order.

Most awards are given to named individuals to be held for life—unless the recipient is discovered to have done something dishonorable, like spying for the Soviet Union or evading paying taxes on a spectacular scale, when he will probably be stripped of it. Emperor Hirohito of Japan was expelled from the Order of the Garter during the Second World War.

One award, introduced in 1966, is for organizations rather than individuals. Harold Wilson, coming to power on a commitment to sweep Britain into the modern world on the tide of a white hot technological revolution, still saw the value of rewards and honours. The Queen's Award to Industry was very much the inspiration of the Labour Government, with the awards made by the Queen on the advice of the prime minister assisted by an advisory committee. Even so, it was a conscious decision to link the awards closely to the sovereign, rather than to the government.

Today, the Queen's Awards for Technological Achievement and for Export Achievement are firmly established as a showcase for British industry. The awards are announced on the Queen's birthday in April. The companies and organizations which are awarded them hold them for five years and may carry the emblem, incorporating a crown, on their stationery and fly its flag outside their premises. The award itself is presented at the company premises by the Lord Lieutenant, the

Queen's representative in the county, and three people from the company are invited to a reception for the year's winners given by the Queen and the Duke of Edinburgh at Buckingham Palace.

The Queen, besides being Sovereign of all nine of the British Orders of Knighthood, has also had conferred upon her the premier orders of many of the foreign countries to which she has made state visits, and protocol demands that she should wear their regalia or ribbons on subsequent visits.

### 1960s GRAND FINALE

The last year of the 1960s was remarkable for two events, one of which changed the world's perception of the Queen, and one of which brought the high drama of a full-blown piece of royal pageantry to a quiet town in North Wales. First came the splendid television documentary, *Royal Family*, then a week later, the Investiture of the Queen's heir, Prince Charles, as Prince of Wales.

Both events were the result of months of planning and hard work behind the scenes. While the Queen had known for some years that one day there would be an investiture for the Prince of Wales, with only the date needing to be decided, the very idea of being put at the centre of a

television film about her life and work horrified her, and it took much persuasion mainly, we are told, from Earl Mountbatten and Prince Philip, to get her to agree. In the event, as the final film demonstrated, the Queen came to enjoy the whole project. The film was hugely successful, being watched by 23 million people in the United Kingdom on its first showing and later by audiences in 130 countries. The success was partly due to the good script—written by Anthony Jay, later co-writer of *Yes, Minister*, a comedy series which took the lid off the workings of government in Britain—and very much due to the unprecedented view it provided of the life of the Royal Family.

The Queen was seen at work at her remarkably cluttered desk, at diplomatic and other receptions, and at one of her regular weekly meetings with her prime minister, Harold Wilson. With her family, she was shown enjoying a barbecue at Balmoral, decorating the family Christmas tree, and having lunch at Buckingham Palace. She was shown feeding her corgis and driving her younger sons and Princess Margaret's children at Windsor.

The film was shot on 75 days over a period of several months, during which the planning for

FAR LEFT: *A highlight of the Queen's state visit to Austria in May, 1969, was a visit to the famous Spanish Riding School in Vienna, where she was presented with the gift of two horses.*

LEFT: *Members of the Royal Family are particularly keen supporters of Britain's Royal Ballet Company. Here, the Queen meets the company's* prima ballerina assoluta, *Margot Fonteyn, and her partner the Russian dancer Rudolph Nureyev at Covent Garden in 1969.*

BELOW: *The moment of climax at the Investiture of Prince Charles as Prince of Wales in July 1969. The Queen places the crown on her son's head.*

RIGHT: *A moment from the 1969* Royal Family *television film: the Queen talks with her then prime minister, Harold Wilson.*

Prince Charles' Investiture as Prince of Wales was also taking place.

The first Prince of Wales to take part in an investiture was Charles' great-uncle David, later Edward VIII. While he learned enough Welsh to be able to read a short speech at his ceremony, Prince Charles actually took time off from his studies at Cambridge to spend a term at the University College of Wales at Aberystwyth learning to speak Welsh.

The months leading up to the Investiture were marked by violent opposition to it from Welsh Nationalist extremists. There were several bomb blasts in Wales, and two would-be bombers were actually killed when their bomb exploded on the day of the Investiture in July 1969. A 'bomb' under a bridge over the River Dee which the royal train was due to cross turned out to be a hoax and no bomb or, indeed, any violent behaviour, marred the ceremony itself.

Amid spectacular scenes of medieval ceremony, set against the towers and turrets of Caernarvon Castle and witnessed by millions through the medium of television, Prince Charles swore fealty to the Queen, promising to 'become your liegeman of life and limb and of earthly worship'. The Queen placed a newly designed crown on his head, buckled on his sword and helped adjust the ermine-trimmed robe which enveloped him. Thus invested, the Prince was led by his mother to the balcony above the castle's Queen Eleanor Gate and was presented by her to the people of Wales.

The ceremony had been Britain's most spectacular piece of pageantry since the Coronation and was, along with the *Royal Family* film, a highly successful public relations exercise, the main effect of which was to bring the Queen and her family closer to the people.

Despite the increasing violence of the times, which in Wales had seemed to come very close to the Queen indeed, she chose to narrow the distance between herself and other people even more. Instead of sheltering behind a massive police presence or using bullet-proof cars wherever she went, just a few months after the investiture she made her first 'walkabout'—an Australian aboriginal term—in the streets of Wellington, the capital of New Zealand. She chose to stroll about among the people who had come to see her, stopping for a brief chat with several of them, rather than just driving past in her car. Though it gave those charged with her securty nightmares, the 'walkabout' became a regular feature of royal visits from then on.

As Elizabeth II's second decade as Queen drew to a close, the threats of violence to the state did not diminish. Even the State Opening of Parliament was not immune and the 1971 ceremony was preceded by a strict search of the Houses of Parliament and the streets around by police anti-bomb squads and sniffer dogs—a far cry from the Yeoman of the Guard armed with halberds who had for centuries been considered sufficiently up to the task of clearing the building of undesirable strangers.

There were occasions, too, when violence was directed, not at the Queen as head of state, but at people or events with which she was associated. The state visit to Britain of Emperor Hirohito of Japan and his Empress in October 1971 aroused considerable hostility. Even Earl Mountbatten of Burma, who had been Supreme Allied Commander

WORLD MILESTONES
1962–1972

**March 1962**
John Glenn, US astronaut, orbits the Earth

**October 1962**
Cuban missile crisis

**June 1963**
Death of Pope John XXIII

**November 1963**
President John F. Kennedy is assassinated in Dallas

**June 1964**
Nelson Mandela sentenced to life imprisonment for treason

**January 1965**
Winston Churchill dies

**June 1965**
US goes on offensive in Vietnam

**June 1966**
Barclays Bank introduces first credit card to Britain

**August 1966**
Cultural revolution begins in China

**June 1967**
Israel defeats Arabs in 6-day War

**August 1968**
USSR crushes 'Prague spring'

**July 1969**
Neil Armstrong becomes first man on the moon

**February 1971**
Decimal currency introduced into Britain

LEFT: *The Queen greets the Emperor and Empress of Japan at the start of their state visit to Britain in October 1971. Emperor Hirohito's visit was not popular with ordinary Britons, but the Queen and the British government saw it as an important exercise in diplomatic bridge-building.*
ABOVE: *The Queen with her Chaplain at the Tower of London after attending Evensong in the Chapel of* *St Peter ad Vincula in the Tower, May 1971. The Chapel is one of several Chapels Royal attached to the Queen. Others are in royal palaces and castles in and near London.*

in the Far East at the end of the war, chose to stay away from the state banquet given in the Emperor's honour, out of respect to all those British and Commonwealth servicemen who had been killed in the Far East or who had become prisoners-of-war of the Japanese.

The Queen clearly felt that the time had come to develop better relations with Japan. At the state banquet she said, 'We cannot pretend that the relations between our two peoples have always been peaceful and friendly. However, it is precisely this experience which should make us all the more determined never to let it happen again.' Even so, her decision to restore to Emperor Hirohito his honorary membership of the Order of the Garter was not popular in Britain.

# The Ceremonies of Monarchy

Ceremony and pageantry play a large part in the life of any head of state, but where the British monarch is concerned, there is probably more of it because the monarchy has been at the head of things for so long: generations of tradition lie behind many of the ceremonies which have become focal points in the royal year.

Some of the ceremonial surrounding the monarchy can easily be seen by anyone taking the trouble to be in the right place at the right time: in front of Buckingham Palace or outside Horse Guards in London in mid-morning to watch the Changing of the Guard, for instance, or in the Jewel House in the Tower of London to see the Crown Jewels, which include the magnificent Coronation Regalia, most of which is used only once in a reign for the greatest ceremonial occasion

of all, the Coronation, though some of it is used in the State Opening of Parliament ceremony.

To be present at an occasion where the Queen herself is involved, surrounded by great ceremonial, is not, in fact, all that easy. Even the large crowd surrounding Horse Guards Parade for Trooping the Colour is there by invitation; without one, the best chance of seeing the Queen is to stand in The Mall and watch her drive past.

The Queen's Birthday Parade, held on the Queen's 'Official' birthday, usually the second Saturday in June, is one of the year's very great occasions, involving 2000 men in magnificent uniforms and 200 horses, all superbly accoutred. The parade attracts thousands of people every year, with many millions more watching it on television.

The parade is a combination of two very old drills, Trooping the Colour and Mounting the Queen's Guard and it has been celebrated in June ever since Queen Victoria instituted the idea of an 'official' birthday at a time more convenient to her subjects than her own birthday.

From the last years of the reign of George VI, when Princess Elizabeth stood in for her sick father, until 1986 the Queen always rode down The Mall at the head of her troops to Horse Guards. Since 1986, she has gone in an open carriage and no longer wears the tunic of the regiment whose colour is being trooped, as she did when she went sidesaddle on horseback to the Parade.

A few days after the Birthday Parade, the Queen may be seen at Windsor Castle —again, mostly by those lucky enough to have obtained spectator tickets—walking in her magnificent Garter robes to St George's Chapel for the annual service of the Most Noble Order of the Garter. This is the oldest order of chivalry in the world and was formed by Edward III in 1348. Its members are a very elite band, indeed; there are only 24 of them, plus the Royal Knights Prince Philip and Prince Charles and several Extra Knights, who are foreign royalty. Edward VII revived an old practice by appointing Ladies of the Garter, and Queen Elizabeth the Queen Mother is the most senior today, having been appointed in 1936.

ABOVE LEFT: *The Queen in robes and plumed hat for the 1971 service of the Order of the Garter.*
LEFT: *The Queen on horseback for the 1968 Trooping the Colour.*
ABOVE RIGHT: *The Royal Maundy service in 1984 took place in Nottingham Cathedral. Here, the Queen holds the traditional posy of sweet-smelling flowers.*
RIGHT: *After many years of riding to Horse Guards Parade for Trooping the Colour, the Queen went in an open carriage for the first time in 1986.*

Both these two great ceremonies will have been preceded in the Queen's year by the service which takes place in one of the great cathedrals of England on Maundy Thursday, the day before Good Friday. This is when she distributes the Royal Maundy—specially minted coins in leather purses—to as many 'good and deserving' men and women as she has years. The ceremony is almost as old as the monarchy itself and orginated in the habit of medieval kings of giving help to the poor while also demonstrating their own humility before God by washing the feet of the poor, as Jesus had washed his disciples' feet.

While the Royal Maundy service has close connections with the Church of England, of which the Queen is head, the State Opening of Parliament is the major ceremonial surrounding the Queen in her role in the political life of the nation. Since the

LEFT: *The Queen wears the Imperial State Crown to read the speech from the throne in the House of Lords during the State Opening of Parliament, 1964.*

ABOVE RIGHT: *The 66th Inter-Parliamentary Conference was held in Westminster Hall, London in September 1975. Here, the Queen is with the British prime minister, Harold Wilson.*

FAR RIGHT: *The Queen and Prince Philip side by side on the thrones in the House of Lords for the 1988 State Opening of Parliament.*

BELOW RIGHT: *The Queen is the first to lay a wreath of poppies at the Cenotaph during the Remembrance Sunday service and parade in Whitehall, November 1978.*

British sovereign's unwritten constitutional right in politics is 'to consult, to encourage and to warn', the speech the Queen reads in the House of Lords is not hers; it has been written by the government of the day and she may not deviate from it. Her presence at the State Opening of Parliament is a symbolic one, emphasizing the continuing workings of a democratically elected government.

For the State Opening of Parliament, the Queen drives down The Mall and along Whitehall to the House of Lords in a splendid procession of horse-drawn carriages, led by Queen Alexandra's State coach carrying the royal Regalia. The Regalia includes the Imperial State Crown, which the Queen puts on when she reaches the House of Lords, the Cap of Maintenance, the Sword of State, and the great Maces. The Queen's carriage is escorted by the Household Cavalry.

Unless there has been a general election earlier in the year, necessitating a special State Opening of Parliament, the ceremony usually takes place early in November, when Parliament assembles for the first time in the winter. This means that within a week or so the Queen will be back in Whitehall for the last and most moving ceremonial occasion of the royal year. On the Sunday nearest 11 November—Armistice Day in 1918—the Queen leads the nation in commemorating the 'Glorious Dead' of two world wars, laying a wreath of

poppies at the foot of the Cenotaph in Whitehall.

With the women members of the Royal Family watching from the balcony nearby, the Queen, the Royal Princes, the Royal Dukes and the prime minister take part in an even more solemn occasion, when servicemen past and present, many of them proudly wearing medals won in battles long ago, march past the Cenotaph. The direct involvement of British troops in two major conflicts in the past ten years has given the ceremony at the Cenotaph in Whitehall, and the annual parade around it, a new significance.

# Family Album
## 1962–1972

The 1960s saw a great enlargement of the Royal Family, with the Queen, her sister Margaret and their cousins the Duke of Kent and Princess Alexandra all having children. The last child of the Queen and Prince Philip, Edward, Anthony Richard Louis, was born in 1964, the same year as the Snowdons' daughter Sarah, the Kents' daughter Helen, and James Ogilvy, son of Princess Alexandra and Mr Angus Ogilvy. (Twenty-one years later, the Queen was to give a splendid ball for all of them at Windsor Castle; closely related, they had also been close to one another since they were born, so it was natural that the whole family should come together to celebrate this milestone in their lives.)

*At Ascot, 1962*

*Charles and Philip at Gordonstoun with Captain Ian Tennant, May 1962*

## FAMILY MILESTONES
### 1962–1972

**June 1962**
Birth of George, Earl of St Andrews, son of the Duke and Duchess of Kent

**April 1963**
Marriage of Princess Alexandra of Kent to Mr Angus Ogilvy

**February 1964**
Birth of James Ogilvy, son of Princess Alexandra and Mr Angus Ogilvy

**March 1964**
Birth of Prince Edward, third son of the Queen and Prince Philip

**April 1964**
Birth of Lady Helen Windsor, daughter of the Duke and Duchess of Kent

**May 1964**
Birth of Lady Sarah Armstrong-Jones, daughter of Princess Margaret

The Queen and Prince Philip were also anxious to heal family wounds at this time. The state visit to Germany in 1965 gave the opportunity for a public display of the Queen's regard for her husband's three sisters. All of them married to German princes, they had not been invited to their brother's wedding in 1947, only two years after the end of the War, but now attitudes towards Germany had changed.

The unveiling of a memorial plaque to Queen Mary in London in 1967 gave the Queen the chance to make a gesture of reconciliation towards the Duke and Duchess of Windsor, who were both invited to attend the ceremony. Hitherto, the Duke, still smarting at the slight to his wife who had never been granted the right to use the style 'Royal Highness', had come to London without her on public occasions. Now, the Duchess was in the front rank at the dedication ceremony, publicly acknowledged by the Queen and the Queen Mother.

Meanwhile for the close members of the Queen's

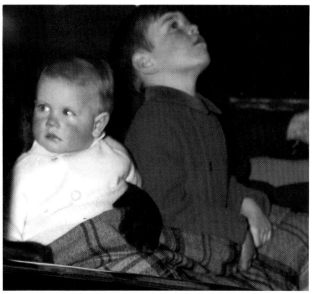

*Edward and Andrew at Liverpool Street Station, 1965*

*A walk in the garden for a family photograph, 1965*

*With Philip's German relations, Salem, May 1965*

family, the old country house at Sandringham was no longer big enough for the traditional family Christmas, and its venue was shifted to Windsor. The Queen and Prince Philip had undertaken much modernizing of the private apartments behind the ancient stone walls of the castle which had been started by William the Conqueror, the result being a friendly and relatively informal household.

While the Queen's 'second family' were still young enough in the 1960s to believe in Father Christmas, her 'first family' were, by the end of the decade, young adults. Prince Charles, having attended his father's old school, Gordonstoun, in Scotland, went to Cambridge to study archaeology and anthropology and, despite taking a term off to study the Welsh language at Aberystwyth, gained an honours degree, the first heir to the throne to do so. For Charles, the decade came to a climax with his Investiture as Prince of Wales.

*A good day out: at a retriever trials day at Balmoral. Lord Porchester is on the left.*

*With Anne at her school, Benenden in Kent, July 1968*

*An informal photograph of the family at Sandringham, just before Charles' Investiture*

Anne, a rather plump and dowdily dressed teenager, emerged from this unpromising chrysalis as a slim, stylish young woman at the end of the decade, making a great impact with the large-brimmed hats she chose to wear, in contrast to the carefully restrained head-hugging headgear favoured by her mother.

To the Queen's delight, Anne also turned out to be a superb horsewoman. Her great interest was three-day eventing, or horse trials, an interest no doubt fostered by the fact that the Badminton Horse Trials, held on the estate of the Queen's Master of the Horse the Duke of Beaufort, had been a regular event on the Royal Family's round throughout Anne's childhood.

In 1971 riding Doublet, a polo pony bred for her father, and competing against most of the best event riders in the world, Anne won the European Three-Day Event Championships at Burghley, in Lincolnshire. The Queen and Prince Philip were both present to witness their daughter's triumph.

*A great day! Anne has just won the European Three-Day Event Championships, 5 September 1971.*

*At Sandringham with a favourite corgi*

# The
# Third Decade

## 1972–1982

ABOVE: *The Queen, wearing the Imperial State Crown.* RIGHT: *The Silver Jubilee Thanksgiving Service in St Paul's Cathedral*

THE THIRD DECADE OF Elizabeth II's reign should have been able to figure in the history books as ten years of unalloyed silver and gold. The decade began for the Queen and Prince Philip with the joyful satisfaction of celebrating 25 years of happy married life and of seeing the first marriage among their children, that of Princess Anne to Captain Mark Phillips in 1973, and ended with the golden splendour of the marriage of their eldest son, Charles, to the Lady Diana Spencer.

In between these three events—family occasions which millions of the Queen's subjects took pleasure in celebrating with her – came that extraordinary outpouring of national and Com-monwealth rejoicing, the Silver Jubilee of the Queen's reign in 1977 and, three years later, the public celebration of the 80th birthday of Queen Elizabeth the Queen Mother.

However, future historians will have to take note of other occasions during the decade which, while they could not quite tarnish the glowing image, would certainly send a few greyish clouds across it.

Foremost among these was the murder of Earl Mountbatten of Burma and his grandson by the IRA in 1979. There were other deaths of people close to the Queen in the 1970s, including her uncle the Duke of Windsor in 1972, her cousin Prince William of Gloucester in a flying accident in 1972,

*'The gift I would most value . . .*
*is that reconciliation should be*
*found wherever needed . . .'*

and Prince William's father the Duke of Gloucester in 1974.

The Duke of Windsor had been ailing for some time and when the Queen, Prince Philip and Prince Charles visited him during a state visit to France in May 1972 he was already dying of cancer. Eight days later the former Edward VIII was dead; the Queen, in sending her condolences to the Duchess, remarked that she was glad she had been able to see him in Paris. An aircraft of the Queen's flight brought the Duke's body to England and the Duchess, a frail, lonely figure, stayed in Buckingham Palace. The Duke's body lay in state at Windsor and was buried at Frogmore.

While the deaths of the two royal dukes, the last surviving children of George V and Queen Mary, were sad events and Prince William's tragic, they were not attended by the dreadful horror with which the life of Earl Mountbatten ended.

Violence had come close to the Queen's family earlier in the decade, with an attempt to kidnap the recently married Princess Anne in London 1974, when her private detective was wounded, and would come again in 1981 with the firing of shots—fortunately, blanks—at the Queen during the Trooping the Colour parade. Once it was quickly seen that all danger was past, these two events, though they resulted in increased security, faded from the minds of Royal Family and public alike, but the murder of Earl Mountbatten left scars that would be long in healing.

The 1970s also saw the first sustained enquiry by Parliament and—inevitably—the press into the royal finances, which had begun in 1969 when Prince Philip had remarked during an interview in America that the Royal Family, the Civil List eroded by inflation, would soon be 'in the red'.

The enquiry into the Civil List was backed up by the Queen's staff at Buckingham Palace with accounts of her public expenses and a detailed survey of what were considered to be the differences between her private and her public expenses. It was accompanied by a good deal of criticism, much of it ill-informed, from MPs, the press and members of the public, many of whom did not see why the Queen should not pay income tax like everyone else. In 1972, an Act of Parliament was passed which not only raised the Civil List—the funds allocated to the Queen for the public duties performed by her and close members of her family—but tied it to Government inflation figures, so that it could be increased automatically with other Government budgets when the country's financial situation warranted it.

Politics in the United Kingdom gave the Queen some difficult moments in the 1970s. One such was the weekend after the Conservative government came through the General Election of February 1974 with some half dozen seats fewer than the Labour Party, when Edward Heath chose not to resign at once but to try to form some sort of an alliance with the minority Liberals. In the end, Heath resigned, and was criticized for not having done so sooner. The Queen had broken off a tour of Australia to fly back to Britain because of the crisis. There was also at least one very unusual moment in

ABOVE LEFT: *The Queen and Prince Charles talking with the Duchess of Windsor outside the Windsors' house in the Bois de Boulogne, Paris, in May 1972. They had just visited the dying Duke of Windsor.*

BELOW LEFT: *The former Edward VIII's funeral took place in St George's Chapel, Windsor, on 5 June 1972. The Queen and the heavily veiled Duchess of Windsor left the chapel together after the service.*

BELOW: *The Queen steps from the royal launch to open the new London bridge spanning the Thames, March 1973.*

British politics when the first woman prime minister came to power in 1979.

It was from Australia, however, that the Queen's most difficult political period would come. Australia, being one of the eleven countries of the Commonwealth of which Elizabeth II is Queen (rather than simply 'Head of the Common-wealth'), has a Governor General, the Queen's personal representative. In 1975 he was Sir John Kerr, who had been appointed on the advice of Australia's prime minister, Gough Whitlam.

By November 1975 Gough Whitlam's position had become difficult in the extreme, with the upper house of the Australian parliament, the Senate, having a majority of opposition members able to block the money bills which came up to them from the lower house, where Whitlam's Labour Party was in a majority.

Even though it began to look as if the administ-

ABOVE: *A rare occasion: the Queen knighted the great West Indian cricketer, Garfield Sobers, in public in Barbados in February 1974.*
LEFT: *The Queen has attended most Commonwealth Games, which are held every four years. Here, she gives out winners' medals at the Games held in Christchurch, New Zealand in 1974.*
RIGHT: *Managing chopsticks with aplomb at a formal dinner during the successful state visit to Japan in 1975*

ration would soon not be able to pay its bills, Gough Whitlam refused to call a general election. Eventually, the Governor General dismissed Whitlam and called on the leader of the opposition, Malcolm Fraser, to become caretaker prime minister pending an election.

Although the Queen did not know of the sudden dismissal of Gough Whitlam and his replacement by Malcolm Fraser until it was all over, it was inevitable that much of the Australian Labour Party's outrage at the way they had been treated by her representative—quite legally, as it happened —spilled over into calls for Australia to become a republic, not a monarchy. Today, Australia is still a monarchy but republicanism remains a plank of Labour Party politics.

The Queen may have reflected on the irony of the fact that her last visit to Australia, had had to be cut short because of the political troubles in the United Kingdom, caused by Edward Heath's decision to call a general election in the midst of a miners' strike. The trip to Australia should have been a pleasant ending to a two-month tour of the South Pacific and the Far East which had included attending the Commonwealth Games in Christchurch, New Zealand.

The next year would see the Queen back in the Pacific, this time making her first state visit to Japan and to the Emperor Hirohito. It was the first such visit by a reigning British monarch to that country, and passed off well. Even better was a visit to Barbados in the West Indies that same year, where the Queen performed the immensely popular act of conferring a knighthood on Garfield Sobers, one of cricket's greatest all-rounders.

### TWENTY-FIVE YEARS A QUEEN

On 6 February 1977 Elizabeth II could look back

WORLD
MILESTONES
1972–1982

**January 1973**
Vietnam ceasefire agreed

**August 1973**
Princess Anne becomes
first member of Royal
Family to visit Russia

**December 1973**
Britain begins a 3-day
week

**August 1974**
President Nixon resigns
over Watergate scandal

**November 1975**
Juan Carlos becomes
King of Spain on death of
Franco

**July 1978**
World's first test tube
baby born

**October 1978**
Polish cardinal elected
Pope as John Paul II

**January/February 1979**
Shah of Iran exiled;
Ayatollah Khomeini
returns to Teheran

**May 1979**
Margaret Thatcher
becomes Britain's first
woman prime minister

**November 1980**
Ronald Reagan becomes
president of US

ABOVE LEFT: *The Queen
inspects the 1st Battalion,
the Grenadier Guards, at
Windsor in April 1976*
BELOW LEFT: *The Queen in
Northern Ireland during her
Jubilee Year*
RIGHT: *The Queen presents
the ladies Singles Trophy to
Virginia Wade at the
Wimbledon Tennis
Championships in 1977. The
cheering was so loud that
Miss Wade could not hear
what the Queen said to her.*

on a quarter of a century as monarch. Already she had occupied the throne longer than her father and great grandfather and only one year less than her grandfather. It seemed a good point at which to give thanks, and a Service of Thanksgiving in St Paul's Cathedral had already been arranged for later in the summer.

Meanwhile, the Jubilee celebrations began in those parts of the Commonwealth where it was already high summer, with the Queen and the Duke of Edinburgh making a seven-week tour of Fiji, New Zealand, Australia and Papua New Guinea in February and March 1977. If the Queen had ever thought that the twenty-fifth anniversary of her accession was going to pass off quietly, the rapturous reception she was given in Fiji must have made her change her mind.

Back in Britain, the Queen began a series of tours round the country which quickly took on the atmosphere of triumphant royal progresses. She began the tours in Glasgow in May, two weeks after she had received loyal addresses from the Lords and Commons in the Palace of Westminster, saying 'I cannot forget that I was crowned Queen of the United Kingdom of Great Britain and Northern Ireland'. It was a pointed reply to the activities of IRA terrorists in Northern Ireland, who had threatened the Queen with violence if she dared set foot in the Province. The point would be made more firmly in August, when the Queen did make a Jubilee visit to Northern Ireland. It was a visit hedged about with far greater security than any of the trips round other parts of the United Kingdom, and there were bombs and shootings while she was there. But Northern Ireland had not become a Royal no-go area, a fact emphasized by the presence of 17-year-old Prince Andrew in the royal party.

By the time summer came round, the United Kingdom seemed to be enjoying one vast Jubilee party. Flag-bedecked street parties became a feature in towns and villages up and down the country and everywhere the Queen went she was fêted by happy crowds. Someone even waved a banner saying 'Great Going, Liz' at the Queen's Birthday Parade on Horse Guards' Parade. For the

first time in some years the Queen went to the Wimbledon Tennis Championship on Ladies' Final day, and inspired Virginia Wade into winning the ladies singles title.

The highlight of Jubilee year in London came on 7 June with the Silver Jubilee Thanksgiving Service at St Paul's, an occasion surrounded by the glitter of royal pageantry at its finest, with the Queen and the Duke of Edinburgh driving to St Paul's in the same golden State Coach they had used for the Coronation.

Later in the month came a Silver Jubilee Review of the Fleet at Spithead. Later still, when things had quietened down somewhat in Britain, there were Jubilee visits to Canada in October and to the Caribbean in November. This was the month when the Queen's first grandchild was born; for the first time that anyone could remember, the Queen was late for an investiture at Buckingham Palace, taking a telephone call to tell her that Princess Anne had given birth to a son.

If anyone thought that the Queen might cut

81

back on her work schedule a little in deference to those 25 action-packed years, they were soon proved wrong. 1978 found her as busy as ever, with a full diary of engagements in the United Kingdom, and a visit to West Berlin forming a part of the 53rd overseas tour of her reign. By now she could list over 100 countries throughout the world that she had visited at least once in her reign, a record that few statesmen in the world could match.

A tour of several Gulf states—Kuwait, Saudi Arabia, Bahrain, Qatar and Oman—early in 1979 was one into unfamiliar territory for the Queen, and for her Islamic hosts. The Queen was careful to travel with a wardrobe of long-skirted, long-sleeved clothes so that she would not offend local sensibilities, but she was also careful to ensure that the skirts were designed so that they could be cut shorter later for wearing in Western countries.

In July 1979 the Queen and the Duke of Edinburgh went to Africa, this time on a tour of Tanzania, Malawi, Botswana and Zambia which also took in the Commonwealth Conference which opened in Lusaka, the capital of Zambia, at the beginning of August. Britain's new prime minister, Margaret Thatcher, had been very doubtful about the wisdom of the Queen's going to Zambia at this time, since guerrillas were using the country as a base from which to attack the government of Bishop Muzorewa in Zimbabwe, and Zimbabwean troops were carrying out counterattacks into Zambia in an effort to destroy the guerrillas' strongholds.

The Queen felt that, as Head of the Commonwealth, she must certainly go to Zambia for the conference. She may also have felt that if it was safe enough for Britain's prime minister to go to the conference, then it was certainly safe enough for her. In the event, a special security team sent out to Zambia reported back that they saw little real danger. The Zimbabwean opposition leader Joshua Nkomo also promised that there would be no guerrilla strikes into Zimbabwe while the Commonwealth Conference was taking place, so the

LEFT: *During an engagement in aid of the 1978 Commonwealth Games Appeal, the Queen and the Duke of Edinburgh visited the BBC and met the cast of the popular television series,* The Good Life: *from the left, Paul Eddington, Penelope Keith, Felicity Kendal and Richard Briars*

ABOVE: *During their tour of
Gulf states in 1979, the
Queen and the Duke of
Edinburgh met the Emir of
Bahrain, Sheikh Isa bin
Salman al Khalifa;
according to British
journalists on the tour with
the Queen, the Emir liked
to be known as 'Jack'.*
RIGHT: *1979 had been
designated the International
Year of the Child; to mark
the Year in Britain, the
'World's Largest Children's
Party' was held in Hyde
Park, London, in May,
with the Queen and Prince
Philip happily mixing with
80,000 children, balloons and
clowns.*

LEFT: *Even the splendour of full naval ceremonial uniform could not hide the sorrow felt by the Prince of Wales and the Duke of Edinburgh as they followed Earl Mountbatten's coffin to his funeral service in Westminster Abbey, 5 September 1979*

BELOW RIGHT: *Black and a head covering are traditional wear for visiting a Pope. The Queen added magnificent diamonds when she went to the Vatican during a state visit to Italy in 1980.*

ABOVE RIGHT: *The moment when teenager Marcus Sarjeant fired a pistol at the Queen as she rode to the Trooping the Colour ceremony in 1981. She quickly brought her horse, Burmese, under control when the mare shied.*

Queen went ahead with the Zambian leg of her tour.

With two arduous tours to the world's hot-spots—climatically and politically—behind her, the Queen went to Balmoral that summer looking forward to several weeks of relaxation surrounded by her family.

A telephone call from the prime minister's office in London on Bank Holiday Monday, 27 August, shattered the tranquillity of the Royal Family's holiday. Earl Mountbatten of Burma, his grandson and a young local boy, taken on as a crewman, had all been killed when a bomb planted by the IRA blew up the Earl's boat in the sea off his holiday home in County Sligo in Eire. Another of Earl Mountbatten's grandsons, his daughter and her husband, Lord Brabourne, were badly hurt and Lord Brabourne's mother died later in hospital.

Lord Mountbatten's state funeral in London on 5 September was for many a time for mourning the whole troubled and divided community in Northern Ireland. Because it was a state funeral, the Queen was at the head of the mourners in Westminster Abbey, her face and those of her family around her expressing their grief at the death of a man who had been Allied Supreme Commander in South-east Asia at the end of the War, and the last Viceroy of India.

Ironically enough, the Queen had probably already pencilled into her diary a visit to the Vatican to meet Pope John Paul II during her state

visit to Italy, planned for October 1980. This was not the first visit to the Vatican to have been made by the Queen, but, despite the factional strife in Northern Ireland, it would pass off with less anti-Catholic comment from some of the Queen's subjects than had earlier ones. Although the Pope had already visited the Irish Republic, his visit to the United Kingdom in return for the Queen's visit to the Vatican would not come for three years, when his meeting with a smiling Queen at Buckingham Palace would be described by the media as 'historic'.

In the meantime, 1980 had a few more pleasant 'historic' moments for the Queen and her family. There was a state visit to Switzerland, the first by a reigning British monarch this century and, back in the United Kingdom, there was the public celebration of Queen Elizabeth the Queen Mother's 80th birthday. Accompanied by her grandson the Prince of Wales, the Queen Mother, smiling happily and looking as if it were her 60th birthday, drove through cheering crowds to join other members of her family and a large congregation in St Paul's Cathedral for a special thanksgiving service on 15 July. More crowds were outside her London home on 4 August, her birthday, to give her flowers and sing 'Happy Birthday'.

By this time the Prince of Wales had already met—in a ploughed field, they both agreed later—the girl who would become his wife, and he had become a literary figure with the publication of his first book. When Queen Victoria had ventured into the world of books, an event which allowed that clever politician Benjamin Disraeli to talk to her about 'We authors, ma'am', she chose to publish an account of her happy life around Balmoral in Scotland. The same setting provided the background for Prince Charles' children's book, *The Old Man of Lochnagar*. The story had begun as a series of bedtime stories for the Prince's younger brothers and now, delightfully illustrated by Sir Hugh Casson, it was one of the more attractive children's books to be published in 1980.

When the author and his family went back to Balmoral for their summer holiday in 1980, among

their visitors was the Lady Diana Spencer, youngest daughter of the Earl Spencer, who had been an equerry to the Queen.

From now until the announcement of their engagement on 24 February 1981, Lady Diana would have to run the gamut of the world's media in full cry, with no help or protection from Buckingham Palace.

The marriage took place in St Paul's Cathedral on 29 July and was another hugely successful royal show. Despite the fact that it was little more than a month since the Queen had been shot at during her birthday Parade, security at the wedding was kept as unobtrusive as possible, the main outward sign of it being the policemen who lined the procession route facing the crowd rather than the procession.

The royal party went to St Paul's and back in open carriages, the bride looked radiant and the groom happily gave her a big kiss on the balcony of

*LEFT: 'Here is the stuff of which fairy tales are made', said the Archbishop of Canterbury in St Paul's on 29 July 1981: the Prince of Wales leads his bride down the aisle after their wedding in the great Cathedral ABOVE: The bride and groom surrounded by their happy families at Buckingham Palace after the wedding ceremony*

Buckingham Palace after the ceremony. Prince Andrew and Prince Edward tied balloons and a 'Just Married' sign on the back of the horse-drawn carriage that took the Prince and Princess of Wales away on their honeymoon, and the Queen threw rose petals after them. It could have been any other happy family wedding—apart from the soldiers with their glittering uniforms, the troops of horses, the presence of many members of Europe's royal houses, and the world-wide television audience estimated at 750 million.

# The Queen and her horses

The Queen's great interest in horses was bred in the bone. Her horse-loving pedigree is as long, if not longer, than the breeding lines of any of her most successful horses. It was Charles II who established the royal interest in horse racing at Newmarket in the seventeenth century, Queen Anne who bought and developed Ascot racecourse (it remains in the Royal Family to this day, being owned by the Queen), and George IV who instituted the daily drive down the course in the royal carriages which is an essential part of the ceremonial of Royal Ascot week.

In another equestrian sporting direction, George V discovered the glories of polo during a stay in Argentina in the 1880s and Edward VIII,

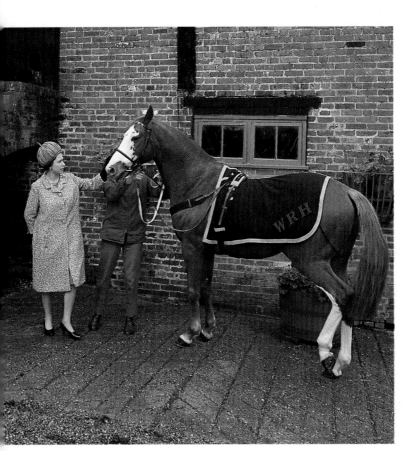

while Prince of Wales, was introduced to the same exciting sport in India in the 1920s. One of the then Princess Elizabeth's first Christmas presents to her new husband was a polo pony, which he used first in Malta when he was stationed there with the Royal Navy.

The Queen is known to have a very good eye for a horse—and not just for racehorses. For several years the huge kettle drums seen in the Queen's Birthday Parade were carried by a splendid horse whose suitability for the job the Queen spotted as soon as she saw him pulling a milk float in Edinburgh.

The young Princess Elizabeth gained her early knowledge of horses from the back of a small pony she was given when she was just three years old (a Shetland, from her royal grandfather). Later, her father introduced her to hunting and, as a girl, she hunted with the famous Pytchley. She began attending race meetings while she was in her teens and was instantly enthralled by everything to do with horseracing—except gambling: she is said never to have had a bet on a horse.

She owned her first horse, Monaveen, with her mother. Monaveen was a steeplechaser and it was not long before the princess and her mother parted ways as owners, Princess Elizabeth concentrating on flat racing, where speed and thoroughbred breeding is all, and her mother devoting herself to National Hunt racing, a winter-time sport over jumps and hurdles, in which she has had considerable success as an owner.

One of Princess Elizabeth's first winning horses was a wedding gift from the Aga Khan. Always able to find witty, unusual names for her horses, she called this filly Astrakhan, and it became a winner for her in 1949.

On George VI's death, his daughter inherited his horses and his studs at Wolferton and Sandringham and she at once set about the task of making them among the most successful racing concerns in the country. By the mid-1950s the Queen was one of Britain's leading owners and in the ten years from 1959 to 1968 she had stake winnings of nearly £160,000.

FAR LEFT: *The Queen with her racehorse Augustine in Sussex, October 1966.*
ABOVE LEFT: *The Queen happily leads in her filly Carrozza after it had won the Oaks at Epsom in 1957. Lester Piggott was the jockey.*
ABOVE RIGHT: *The Queen's horse Magna Carta won the Ascot Stakes Handicap at Royal Ascot in 1970.*
RIGHT: *The Royal Family was out in force to see Mill Reef win the 1971 Derby. Here, the Duke of Edinburgh, Queen Elizabeth the Queen Mother, the Queen and other members of the Royal Family study the horses before the race.*

The great times for the royal stables lasted into the 1980s. Her filly, Dunfermline, won both the Oaks and the St Leger in the Jubilee year of 1977, which meant that she had won every English Classic race with home-bred horses—except the Derby. Her long-time racing manager, the Earl of Carnarvon (formerly Lord Porchester), makes no secret of the fact that it remains the Queen's main ambition to win the greatest English Classic of them all. Her superb horse Aureole has come nearest so far, being beaten by Pinza, with the great Sir Gordon Richards up, in the Coronation year Derby, and she has had no success in the years since. At Sandringham there is a statue of Edward VII's famous Derby winner, Persimmon, to remind her—not that she needs reminding—that

LEFT: *Keeping a record of events at the Royal Windsor Horse Show in 1982.*

BELOW LEFT: *The Queen seldom misses the annual Royal Windsor Horse Show, held in Windsor Great Park. Here, she takes an interest in an event at the 1987 show.*

RIGHT: *The Queen at the annual stallion show of the National Light Horse Breeding Society in March 1984.*

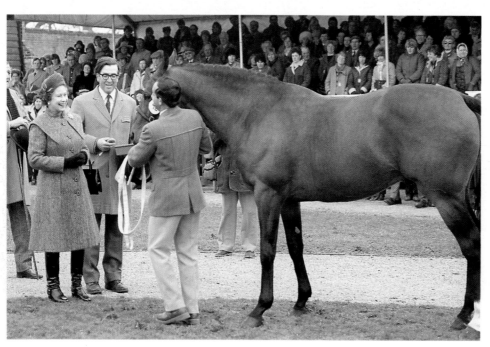

royal horses can and do win Derbies. It just needs perseverence, some luck, the right horse—and a lot of patience and money.

The Queen's money to pay for her horses is earned by the horses themselves, in prize money, judicious selling and stud fees. The royal stables and studs are run along strongly commercial lines, the aim being to make a profit, or at least to break even.

In 1991 the Queen and her racing manager squarely faced the fact that she could not compete with the huge amounts of money from Arab owners who now dominated British racing. It was announced that over the next two seasons, therefore she would reduce her string of racehorses from the current 36 thoroughbreds in training at any one time (a leading Arab owner at the time, Sheikh Muhammad had 337 in training) down to 25. In so doing she would effectively take herself out of the list of the top twenty racehorse owners in Britain.

In breaking the news, however, Lord Carnarvon made it clear that she would remain an outstandingly skilled breeder as well as an owner, and would be going for quality, not quantity, with that elusive Derby winner still very much in mind. She would undoubtedly still be making full use of the computer given to her in California by Ronald Reagan and his wife which has a direct link to Kentucky where the Queen actively breeds thoroughbreds—she often has up to half a dozen mares in foal there at any one time.

The Queen's interest in horses extends beyond the specialist world of racehorses. Although it was undoubtedly pride in her daughter's achievement in winning the European Three-Day Event championships in 1971 that spurred her into commissioning the statuette of Princess Anne on Doublet which now sits on her desk at Buckingham Palace, it should not be forgotten that Doublet was the Queen's horse, bred originally as a polo pony for Prince Philip.

The Queen's interest in show jumping—she was partowner of an Olympic horse, Countryman, in the 1950s—and in three-day eventing, or horse trials, has been long-standing and keen. She seldom

misses the Royal Windsor Horse Show, an annual event in which show jumping and carriage driving, Prince Philip's great interest in his later years, are paramount.

Her attendance at the Badminton Horse Trials year after year during Princess Anne's girlhood must have done much to spur her daughter's interest in the sport, while the whole family's close interest in Prince Philip's polo-playing activities through the years must surely have done much to promote the Prince of Wales' keen interest in polo today.

The Queen has often been quoted as saying that if she had not been destined to be Queen she would have liked to live in the country with lots of horses and lots of dogs. As it has turned out, she has managed to combine both ways of life more than satisfactorily.

*A photograph taken at Balmoral to mark the Silver Wedding anniversary*

*The whole family celebrates the silver wedding*

# *Family Album*
## 1972–1982

The third decade of the Queen's reign contained both good times and bad times for her family.

The first year of the decade had both, for it saw both the death of the Duke of Windsor in May and the celebration of the silver wedding anniversary of the Queen and the Duke of Edinburgh in November.

To mark the latter, there was a service of thanksgiving in Westminster Abbey, followed by a light-hearted celebratory lunch at the Guildhall in the City of London. While these were public events, the family nature of the silver wedding was emphasized in the official photographs issued at the time, which showed the Queen and Duke together and with their children.

The great family occasion of 1973 was the marriage of the Queen and Prince Philip's only daughter Anne to Captain Mark Phillips. The independent princess had gone outside the royal circle for her husband, for Mark Phillips was someone she had come to know through her riding

*Anne and Mark engaged: photographed in the Long Gallery, Windsor Castle*

*A 50th birthday photograph, Windsor Castle 1976*

*Anne with the horse she rode at the Montreal Olympics*

*The christening of Peter Phillips, December 1977*

interests. She had known him for some years: alert viewers of the *Royal Family* television film would have seen her in lively conversation with him at a reception for the British Olympics team in the late 1960s. Mark Phillips, serving in the Queen's Dragoons, was also a very successful three-day event rider and a member of the British Olympic team in 1972.

Their marriage took place on 14 November 1973 in Westminster Abbey. The princess did not want to be surrounded by hordes of children at her wedding, so there were only two to follow her and her father up the aisle to where Mark awaited her— her brother Edward and her cousin Sarah Armstrong-Jones. For the Royal Family, the wedding was a day of great happiness and pleasure; for many ordinary Britons it was a last gleam of light before the gloom cast by a miners' strike and prime minister Edward Heath's response to it, the notorious three-day week.

Marriage proved no hindrance to the princess's riding career and by 1976 she had proved so good in her chosen sport that she was included in the British three-day event team for the Olympic Games in Montreal. When she went to Canada, her husband and her parents went, too. The Queen was there as Queen of Canada but she was also there as Anne's proud and supportive mother.

Another member of the Queen's family in need of her support at this time was her sister Margaret, whose marriage to the Earl of Snowdon, unhappy for some years, was now clearly over, barring the formalities. The question in royal circles was just what form the 'formalities' would take. With the Queen's cousin, the Earl of Harewood, having been divorced in 1967, divorce was no longer unthinkable in the Royal Family; in 1976 the Snowdons' separation was announced, to be followed by divorce two years later.

Between these two sad dates, the Queen's own family had happily increased: she had become a grandmother. In November 1977, Princess Anne gave birth to a boy, who was christened Peter Mark Andrew at Buckingham Palace in December, just before the family all went off to Windsor for the Christmas

*With Queen Elizabeth the Queen Mother on her 80th birthday*

*With Charles and Diana at Buckingham Palace*

gathering. The Phillips' 'pigeon pair' was completed with the birth of their daughter Zara Anne Elizabeth in May 1981.

Although the Queen took a great interest in her first two grandchildren, there was never any question of their being introduced into the royal round. Princess Anne, like her aunt Margaret, has always insisted that her children are not royal and that, despite their very royal grandmother, they will grow up as private citizens.

Despite the grief caused in the Royal Family by the murder of their 'Uncle Dickie' Mountbatten in 1979, the decade actually ended on a very high note.

First of all, there was the Queen Mother's 80th birthday, celebrated in public with a service of thanksgiving in St Paul's and in private with a big family party.

Then in 1981 came the marriage of the Prince of Wales to Lady Diana Spencer.

The wedding in St Paul's Cathedral was a sumptuous blend of religious observance and magnificent music. Where the Queen at her wedding had promised 'to love, honour and obey' her husband, Diana chose the more modern marriage vow which did not include 'obey'.

As with Anne's wedding, that of the Queen's eldest son managed to combine pageantry with fun and informality – a true family wedding.

*At Sandringham just before the 30th anniversary of the accession*

# The
# Fourth Decade

## 1982 – 1992

THE QUEEN'S THOUGHTS, IF not her actions, were dominated by events in the South Atlantic during the first year of the fourth decade of her reign. History books call Britain's fight with Argentina for possession of the Falkland Islands a 'conflict', not a war: the United Kingdom's Supreme Commander of the Armed Forces was not required to sign an Order in Council declaring her country at war with Argentina. Still, many thousands of men of whose regiments she was Colonel-in-Chief, or for whom she was Lord High Admiral or Commandant-in-Chief were involved in the 'conflict', including her son Prince Andrew, a helicopter pilot in the Royal Navy.

ABOVE: *The Queen in Garter robes.*
RIGHT: *Celebrating the 250th anniversary of Downing Street with Mrs Thatcher.*

The first intimation of trouble in the South Atlantic reached the British public towards the end of March 1982, with reports that a group of Argentinians, apparently collecting scrap from an old whaling station, had hoisted their country's flag on the island of South Georgia. A Royal Navy patrol ship, the *Endurance*, was speeding to investigate.

By the end of the first week in April, Britain had broken off diplomatic relations with Argentina, the Foreign Secretary, accepting responsibility for 'a very great national humiliation', had resigned and the prime minister, Mrs Thatcher, had sent a Task Force off to the South Atlantic to restore the

*'A constitutional monarchy excels all other forms of government . . . It is not only a symbol of unity, but you respect and admire the monarch as well.'*

Falkland Islands to British rule. Leading the Task Force from Portsmouth on 5 April were the carriers *Hermes* and *Invincible*, on which Prince Andrew was serving.

Ten days after the Task Force had sailed, the Queen left London for Canada; despite the conflict, it was to be business as usual. In Canada, the Queen attended ceremonies marking the country's adoption of a new constitution, and she signed with a flourishing 'Elizabeth R' the proclamation of Canada's final independence from the overlordship of Parliament in Britain. Although she was only in Canada a few days, the Queen had a hot-line to Downing Street in case of any escalation in the Falkland crisis.

The following month in England came that 'historic' meeting with Pope John Paul II. The Pope came to Buckingham Palace in his white 'Popemobile' and had a 35-minute meeting alone with the Queen. There was an exchange of gifts, the Queen giving the Polish-born Pope a leather-bound facsimile of a Sobieski Book of Hours in the Royal Library at Windsor, and the Pope giving the Queen a silver bas-relief of Christ on the Cross. As he left, the Pope told the Queen 'I will pray for your son in the Falklands.'

Since there was no hot-line to HMS *Invincible*, this was all that the Queen herself could do for her son and the rest of the Task Force. When she had been asked during a visit to Manchester how Andrew was, all she could reply, like any other mother whose son was involved in the fighting, was 'I hope he is all right'. It was probably just as well that she did not find out till later that one of her son's tasks in the Falklands had been to fly his helicopter as a decoy for Exocet missiles fired at British ships: there was no cottonwool treatment for the Queen's son in the South Atlantic.

LEFT: *The Queen talks to Chelsea Pensioners during the celebrations marking the 300th anniversary of the Royal Hospital, Chelsea.*
RIGHT: *HMS Invincible is home from the Falklands, and Prince Andrew's mother has come to greet him and his shipmates; his father and sister were there, too.*
BELOW RIGHT: *The Queen visits the Temperate House at Kew Gardens, May 1982.*

## THE REAGANS AT WINDSOR

Helping to keep the Queen's mind off things in the Falklands in early June were the President of the United States and Mrs Reagan. They arrived in England on 7 June, and spent an enjoyable few days at Windsor Castle, where on their first evening there was a quiet dinner party attended by several other members of the Royal Family, including the Princess of Wales whose first baby was due in two or three weeks' time. The next day the Queen and President Reagan went riding in Windsor Home Park and Prince Philip took Mrs Reagan for a carriage drive. Later, the President and Mrs Reagan went up to London, where the President addressed members of both houses of Parliament in the Royal Gallery of the Palace of Westminster. The day ended with the formal magnificence of a banquet in Windsor Castle.

An important event in the Queen's Diary after the Reagans had left was the Founder's Day parade at the Royal Hospital, Chelsea. Every year, a member of the Royal Family or a leading service commander takes the salute at this parade of those very special old soldiers, the Chelsea Pensioners, but 1982 was the tercentenary of the founding of the Hospital by Charles II, and the Queen took the

salute herself. She also attended a reception at the Royal Hospital and visited the infirmary, so that those soldiers not well enough to attend the parade could meet their sovereign.

### GOOD TIMES AND BAD

By mid-June, British troops had regained the Falkland Islands and the Queen's Press Secretary was able to say that the Queen was 'delighted and relieved' at the news, though saddened by the tragic loss of life. She was also able to send a quick message to everyone in the Falklands via Prince Andrew, who unexpectedly telephoned her at Windsor from a Royal Fleet Auxiliary anchored in Stanley Harbour. It would not be until September that the Queen and Duke of Edinburgh would be able to see their son personally, when *Invincible* arrived home in Portsmouth to a tumultuous welcome. Prince Andrew, a rose between his teeth, cheered as happily as everyone else.

Thus, there was no Falklands worry to cloud the Queen's joy at the birth of the first child of the

Prince and Princess of Wales on 21 June. The baby, a boy, was born, not in a palace, but in a large London hospital, St Mary's Paddington, and Prince Charles, a properly modern father, was present at the birth. The Queen saw her third grandchild within a day of his birth and was present at his baptism, when he was given the names William Arthur Philip Louis by the Archbishop of Canterbury at Buckingham Palace on 4 August, the 82nd birthday of the baby's great-grandmother, the Queen Mother.

Between these two happy occasions, came other events which considerably distressed the Queen. Despite Buckingham Palace's supposedly excellent security, an intruder managed to make his way right into the Queen's bedroom early one morning in July. Clutching a broken ashtray and bleeding from a self-inflicted cut, Michael Fagan sat on the Queen's bed for some time before she was able to summon help. Even then, it was a chambermaid (whose cry of 'Bloody hell, ma'am, what's he doing here?' would become famous) and the young footman who had been giving the Queen's corgis their early morning walk, rather than the palace police, who would do most to help the Queen get the dishevelled Fagan out of her bedroom and into a pantry where they kept him until the police, who had ignored a burglar alarm, the Queen's bedside alarm bell and two telephone calls from her, finally appeared on the scene.

Two weeks later, a troop of the Queen's

personal guards from the Blues and Royals was blown up by an IRA bomb in Hyde Park and the band of the Royal Green Jackets was the target of another bomb in Regent's Park. Composed and courageous in public, in private the reality was that the Queen was deeply shaken by these events and would take several months to recover from them.

BELOW LEFT: *When the Queen visited the Sue Ryder home at Snettisham in Norfolk in February 1983, one of the residents showed her the jigsaw puzzle of the Prince of Wales' wedding she had been doing.*
LEFT: *Since modern shopping centres play such a big part in ordinary folks' lives, it is entirely appropriate that someone as important as the Queen should officially open them; the one being opened here in March 1983 is at Ealing in West London.*
RIGHT: *The Queen with President Reagan at Santa Barbara Airport during her visit to California in March 1983.*

### ABROAD IN 1983

The Queen and the Duke of Edinburgh had two major trips abroad in 1983. First came a trip to visit President Reagan at his ranch and to carry out other engagements in California. This was not a state visit, as the Queen's trip to the US in 1976, the year of the Bicentennial, had been. This was a more relaxed occasion, almost a holiday – except that the weather was dreadful. The President's gift to the Queen on the occasion was appropriate, given that they were in the heartland of American computer technology: a computer into which she could programme the bloodlines of her thoroughbreds. But other things are more important to the Queen than her racehorses, and President Reagan's stock with her would drop somewhat later in the year when he sent American troops to Grenada, a West Indian island within the Commonwealth.

The Queen and Duke of Edinburgh's visit to India later in the year was a more formal affair. Mrs Indira Gandhi, once more in power as prime minister, had been in London for the launching of a major Festival of India in March 1982, when she had lunched with the Queen. Now, she was the Queen's main hostess in India. Both she and Mother Teresa, whom the Queen met in India, featured in that year's Christmas Broadcast, in which the Queen emphasized the importance of the Commonwealth's role in world affairs. Months later, Mrs Gandhi was assassinated.

FAR LEFT: *A particularly important engagement on the Queen's tour of India in 1983 was her meeting with Mother Teresa, who was made an honorary member of the Order of Merit by the Queen in 1983.*

LEFT: *In 1985 No. 10 Downing Street had been the residence of Britain's prime minister for 250 years. The Queen joined six of her prime ministers to celebrate the occasion at Downing Street; from the left: Lord Callaghan, Sir Alec Douglas-Home, Mrs Margaret Thatcher, the Earl of Stockton (Harold Macmillan), Lord Wilson and Mr Edward Heath.*

WORLD MILESTONES
1982–1992
**April 1982**
Falklands invaded
**March 1984**
Nationwide miners' strike begins in Britain
**January 1986**
US space shuttle explodes; all on board die
**April 1986**
USSR reactor tragedy at Chernobyl
**April 1989**
Students demonstrate in Peking
**November 1989**
The Berlin Wall opens
**November 1990**
Margaret Thatcher ousted as prime minister; John Major takes her place
**February 1991**
Gulf War begins

## D-DAY 1984

The fortieth anniversary of the D-day landings which marked the beginning of the end of the Second World War, fell in 1984. In Normandy in June, the Queen led British participation in the events celebrating the anniversary.

The day began with ceremonies at Caen and Bayeux, two towns which had borne the brunt of the fighting in 1944, and on the stretch of flat, sandy coastline still sign-posted with the name it had been given on the invasion maps—Utah Beach. Here, eight leaders of the nations which had been involved in the Allied cause in 1944—Presidents Reagan of the USA and Mitterand of France, Pierre Trudeau of Canada, King Baudouin of the Belgians and King Olav of Norway, Grand Duke Jean of Luxembourg and two queens, Beatrix of the Netherlands and Elizabeth—lined up to salute the young troops from the nations' present fighting forces who paraded before them.

Later, the Queen presided over a British ceremony at Arromanches, where several thousand veterans of World War II marched past her to the soldiers' version of 'Colonel Bogey'. As she reminded them in her speech, they were marking the anniversary of 'one of the few occasions in history when the course of human destiny has depended on the events of a single day'. The speeches over, the Queen and her husband were able to walk freely among the veterans, stopping to talk with them and share their memories of World War II.

The Queen could not be so relaxed and untroubled by strict security everywhere else in the brave new world of the 1980s. The contrast between the visit to Normandy and a visit to Jordan in the same year was marked. The Jordan visit nearly did not take place at all, so volatile was the situation in the Middle East. There had been bomb blasts in the capital, Amman, and other scares elsewhere. But King Hussein telephoned the prime minister, personally guaranteeing the Queen's safety and, in the end, she went, in a British Airways aircraft fitted with missile-deflection equipment.

Amman airport looked as if it were beseiged, so great were the numbers of armed guards, machine guns at the ready. The Queen was swept into a bullet-proof car and driven at speed into Amman, surrounded by an armed escort. It was all very unsettling. But the visit passed off well, with no serious incidents, and was seen by the British Foreign Office as a very good piece of foreign relations.

There was another trip abroad in 1984, this time to Canada, and this time the Queen and the Duke of Edinburgh went as grandparents four times over: the second son of the Prince and Princess of Wales, Henry Charles Albert David—but always known as Harry—was born in London in September.

The Canadian visit over, the Queen popped over the border into the United States for a private visit to some of the best studs and racehorse breeding establishments in Kentucky and Wyoming. She was on a ranch in Wyoming when news reached her from England of the IRA bomb which had partially destroyed the Grand Hotel in Brighton where many members of the Conservative Party

106

LEFT: *The wartime allies France and Britain were represented by President Mitterand and Elizabeth II at the 40th anniversary of the D-day celebrations in France, June 1984.*
RIGHT: *The Queen and her two eldest sons at the unveiling of the memorial to the South Atlantic Campaign in St Paul's Cathedral, June 1985. This was a more low-key affair than had been the Falkland Islands Service in July 1982, also in St Paul's. Many people saw the latter as an attempt to glorify the conflict, rather than to mourn the dead.*

were staying during their annual party conference. The prime minister and her husband escaped injury by a hairsbreadth, but others did not. In that same month Indira Gandhi was assassinated in India. No longer could the Queen consider herself an unlikely target for assassination, as she had so serenely felt at the beginning of her reign.

Back in England, a visit from President Mitterand of France, the State Opening of Parliament and the Remembrance Service at the Cenotaph in Whitehall were all surrounded by heightened levels of security, though the Queen was always insistent that it should be as unobtrusive as possible.

Indeed, there were still many occasions when security could be very light. Prince Harry's christening was one such. It took place at Windsor a few days before Christmas, in time for film of the occasion to add some charmingly light-hearted moments to the Queen's Christmas broadcast that year.

Throughout the middle years of the 1980s, the Queen continued in her public and her private life much as she had always done. The annual ceremonies, the state visits, the local events at home and abroad, were carried out along lines she had established long before her staff had needed to worry about bombs, terrorists and madmen. When her second son, Andrew, married the red-haired and exuberant Miss Sarah Ferguson in the summer of 1986, they drove to their wedding in Westminster Abbey in horse-drawn carriages, with the crowds allowed close enough to see them well—as royal newly married couples traditionally had always done.

### BEHIND THE WALL

For much of the post-World War II period, China had been an unknown quantity in the world, closed to Western influence. In the 1970s Chinese attitudes to the rest of the world changed and the country's leaders began to look outwards. US President Richard Nixon's greatest achievement while in office was the building up of a good American relationship with China. Soon, other Western nations followed in his footsteps. By the mid-1980s the time was right for Elizabeth II to pay a visit.

She had been to the British colony of Hong Kong, of course, and during her 1975 Far East tour had looked over the fence, as it were, into the land of Hong Kong's huge neighbour. But now, in October 1986, the Queen and the Duke of Edinburgh found themselves in the very heart of China.

There was the usual round of official receptions, enabling the Queen and the British government officials in her train to get to know the people in power in China, and there were numerous opportunities to meet at least a few of China's more ordinary citizens in many different parts of that large and very enigmatic country.

The Queen and her party visited the old Imperial City of Peking, the Forbidden City, and walked along a section of the extraordinarily impressive Great Wall of China. Perhaps most memorable of all was a visit to the burial site of China's first emperor, Qin Shi Huangdi, the man who had had the Great Wall built.

The burial site was found by accident in 1974, near Mount Li in north-west China. Carefully

ABOVE: *The Queen attends a state banquet at Kunming, capital of Yunnan province in the south of China.*

RIGHT: *Like most other tourists from the West, the Queen and the Duke of Edinburgh walked along a stretch of the Great Wall during their visit to China in October 1986.*

excavated, the site revealed 7000 life-size terracotta figures of soldiers with their attendant chariots and horses, all lined up to maintain a vigil round the body of the emperor, who died in 210BC. Even the Queen, who had seen many amazing sights in thirty five years of touring all over the world, looked awed as she walked among these wonderfully delicately carved figures standing in battle formation.

## FORTY YEARS ON

As the Queen neared the end of her fourth decade as monarch she came to seem more and more a point of stability in a rapidly changing world. Her waistline might be less slender than once it had been and her hair greyer, but that was only right and proper in a woman who celebrated her 40th wedding anniversary in 1987 and whose sixth grandchild was born in 1990.

It also seemed right and proper in a monarch, as the President of Poland, Lech Walesa, indicated when he came to Britain on a state visit in 1991. The former shipyard trade union leader, sent on the great wave of changes caused by the historic collapse of communist regimes throughout Eastern Europe to the head of his country's government, had much admiration to express both for the stabilizing effect of the institution of monarchy in a democracy and for the monarch herself.

He also made jokes about the vastness of the bed he and his wife were given to sleep in at Windsor Castle, which everyone took as an indication of the miraculously right way things were going in Eastern Europe: no more grey, hard-faced commissars, just ordinary, decent men and women.

*A wide variety of events fills the Queen's diary every year. Here is a representative selection from 1987:*
ABOVE LEFT: *The Scots Guards are presented with new colours by their Colonel-in-Chief, the Queen, at Buckingham Palace;*
LEFT: *The Queen with King Hassan of Morocco, on a state visit to Britain, in return for the state visit the Queen made to Morocco in 1980.*

Vaclav Havel, the President of Czechoslovakia, who had also recently visited Britain, was seen as another in the same mould, though his leanings were more intellectual, since he was famous as a playwright before he became his country's president.

As for the Queen, she greeted the new presidents of Poland and Czechoslovakia and the communist president of the Soviet Union, Mikhail Gorbachev who came to Britain in 1989, in the same way and with the same ceremony and same order of events for their stay as she had been doing for all state visitors for four decades. And she carried out her visits abroad, including Portugal in 1985, the Netherlands in 1989 (a very special visit, marking the Tercentenary of the Glorious Revolution of 1689 which had brought William of Orange to the throne of England), Iceland in 1990, the United States in 1991, as well as one or two of the countries of the Commonwealth most years, in the same spirit of friendly interest she had been showing for those same four decades.

If there was any change in the way the Queen approached things it lay in her more relaxed attitude. She was ready to make a few jokes of her

*ABOVE RIGHT: The Duke of Gloucester, Grand Prior of the Order of St John of Jerusalem greets his cousin, the Queen, as she arrives to attend the St John Ambulance Centenary celebration in Hyde Park;*
*RIGHT: Fine examples of Roman glass are inspected by the Queen at the 'Caesar's Glass' exhibition at the British Museum.*

LEFT: *President Gorbachev of the USSR made a state visit to Britain in 1989. He and his wife, Raisa, spent some days at Windsor Castle as guests of the Queen and the Duke of Edinburgh.*

own, even on formal occasions. In Washington in 1991 she became the first reigning British sovereign to address a joint session of the United States Congress and she had her audience laughing and clapping before she began her speech simply by remarking dryly, 'I do hope you can see me today from where you are.' It was a reference to the fact that on her arrival in Washington President George Bush had put her behind a lectern so tall that when she made her reply to his speech of welcome all that the audience could see of her was her striped hat.

This is not to say that the Queen did not take a serious view of the importance of her visits abroad. Far from it. As she said in another speech in America, 'There is a symbolism in such a visit which defies analysis but which reaches to peoples far and wide.' That her visit to the United States in 1991 was a symbol of the relationship between the US and the UK she emphasized when she made General Norman Schwarzkopf—'Stormin' Norman' who had led the allied forces in the Gulf War against Saddam Hussein earlier in the year—an honorary Knight Companion of the Bath.

The Queen was not the only head of state to be welcomed to Washington in 1991, but her visit

aroused the most interest. Her visits to an underprivileged suburb in Washington – where her laughter at being hugged by a very large lady in a Washington apartment was seen round the world courtesy of television and newspapers—to a baseball game (her first), to the Alamo, and to many other places of interest in Texas and Miami made news in America and abroad. To Americans, the queen is not just another head of state, she is an international star; she has been one, not for Andy Warhol's 15 minutes, but for four decades.

Sometimes, now that she has passed 'retirement' age—she was 65 in 1991—people in Britain suggest that she might like to consider putting her feet up, as it were, to spend more time with her family, her horses and her corgis—to abdicate, in fact. This is to miss an essential point. The Queen is not a company chairman who has reached her current eminent position through promotion and hard work. She was annointed and crowned Queen in a religious ceremony that emphasized that the crowning was for life.

One more decade to go, and the Queen and her millions of subjects will be able to celebrate her Golden Jubilee. She will still be an international star and we will still say 'Long may she reign'.

RIGHT: *The Queen and the penguins inspect each other at London Zoo.*

BELOW: *The christening of Princess Eugenie, second daughter of the Duke and Duchess of York, took place at Windsor Castle in December 1990. Pictured at the christening: the Duke and Duchess of York (with Eugenie), the Queen, Princess Margaret, the Princess Royal, the Princess of Wales and her sons William and Harry.*

# Prince Philip

When the Queen's husband celebrated his 70th birthday in 1991, one national newspaper, marking the occasion with a series of articles surveying his place in British public life, remarked that 'Britain is unimaginable without Prince Philip'.

For the forty years of Elizabeth II's reign, Prince Philip has always been there, fulfilling the difficult, because undefined, role of prince consort to perfection, always at her side for the great ceremonial state occasions, always accompanying her on state visits and royal tours overseas. At home, we are told, Prince Philip is very much the head of the family, a devoted, if not entirely uncritical, father interested in the affairs of all his children, though

ABOVE: *An official portrait of the Duke of Edinburgh, taken in 1985.*
LEFT: *Action Man on a bicycle: a leading charity benefitted from this vigorous game of bicycle polo in 1967.*
RIGHT: *Prince Philip getting his team through a difficult obstacle in a driving event in 1983. Carriage driving is now his principal sporting activity.*

perhaps closest to his daughter Anne. He has been the man in charge of the Royal Family's private estates, turning Sandringham into an efficient and profitable business quite early in the Queen's reign. But, above all, Prince Philip has looked on his position as consort to the Queen as the most important part of his life and work.

Prince Philip was born on the Greek island of Corfu on 10 June 1921, the son of Prince Andrew of Greece and his wife Princess Alice of Battenburg. When he was born, the baby, whose full name was Philippos Schleswig-Holstein-Sonderburg-Glucksberg, was sixth in line to the Greek throne. As his mouthful of a name indicates, he was also related to most of the royal houses of Europe; his own family's origins were Danish, and they were also descended from Queen Victoria.

When Philip first met his young third cousin, Princess Elizabeth, at the Royal Naval College at Dartmouth, he already had a largely British education behind him. He had been at a prep school in England and spent several years at Gordonstoun in Scotland, where he became Head Boy and captain of cricket and hockey. Early in World War II he was commissioned into the Royal Navy, and it was as plain naval lieutenant Philip Mountbatten that his engagement to George VI's elder daughter was announced in 1947.

On the day before his wedding, Philip was created Duke of Edinburgh by George VI, who announced that the young man would also be permitted to use the prefix 'His Royal Highness'. The King seems to have believed that this title automatically carried with it the style of 'Prince', but, in fact, the Queen's husband had to wait another ten years before the Queen made him a

Merit. He has high-ranking appointments in all three of the armed services and is patron or president of many national and international organizations, foremost among them being the World Wide Fund for Nature (formerly the World Wildlife Fund) and his own Duke of Edinburgh Award Scheme. His interests, pursued with vigour and concern, centre on environmental matters, the welfare of young people, and the place of science and technology in the world.

He has been an internationally successful sportsman in several fields, notably sailing, polo and carriage driving, a sport he took up in middle age when wrist trouble meant he could no longer play polo. He pilots his own aircraft and likes driving fast cars. He was, in fact, a true 'Action Man' before the media gave the title to his eldest son, Charles. Philip is also a better-than-amateur painter whose eye for a good picture has led to some notable additions being made to the royal art collection. He has written several books, most notably one about the birds he saw from the royal yacht *Britannia* during two long cruises in southern oceans and

Prince of the United Kingdom.

Just before the birth of their second son, Andrew, in 1960, the Queen also brought her husband's surname out of the oblivion into which it had been cast at the outset of her reign. An announcement in Council made it clear that her descendants, other than those enjoying the style 'Royal Highness', would bear the surname 'Mountbatten-Windsor'. The Queen had chosen to do this, the announcement made clear, because she 'has always wanted, without changing the name of the Royal House established by her grandfather, to associate the name of her husband with her own and his descendants. The Queen has had this in mind for a long time and it is close to her heart.' Princess Anne's marriage certificate named her as 'Anne Elizabeth Alice Louise Mountbatten-Windsor', despite the fact that she was also a 'Royal Highness'.

Today, Prince Philip is a Knight of the Garter and a Knight of the Thistle. He has been a Privy Councillor since 1951 and he holds the Order of

Antarctica during the 1950s.

His outspoken manner and somewhat acerbic wit earned him some notoriety in the early years of the reign; today, perhaps mellowed by the passing years, Prince Philip is seen to be more often right than wrong in his public pronouncements—of which there have been many, for he has never been content to be simply a supportive figure in the Queen's shadow. Often, it has seemed as if he has deliberately set out to say things which the Queen's position does not allow her to say, but which he feels ought to be said—and said by someone who may be seen as a sort of national, politically unbiased, cheer-leader.

Today, perhaps slightly overshadowed by the careers of his very active children and their growing families, Prince Philip has earned the right to sit back a little. After all, his was very much the guiding hand that steered the Royal Family through the difficulties of a rapidly-changing twentieth century and gave an old-fashioned and, some would say, out-dated institution a positive and essential place in the life of the nation.

ABOVE LEFT: *The Duke of Edinburgh accompanies the Queen to the annual service of the Order of the Garter in 1958.*
BELOW LEFT: *The Duke makes friends with a panda during the royal tour of China in 1986; he has been a leading figure in the Worldwide Fund for Nature for many years.*
ABOVE RIGHT: *A good view of the opening ceremonies of the Commonwealth Games in New Zealand in 1974.*
BELOW RIGHT: *Acerbic wit meets brilliant comedy: the Duke of Edinburgh with Eric Morcambe in 1973.*

# *Family Album*

## 1982 – 1992

In the 1980s the Queen's family grew and its members' lives changed and moved in sometimes surprising directions, just as do those of any family group anywhere, though with a burden of overwhelming media attention that few other families have had to contend with.

It must sometimes have seemed to the Queen that the media would choose just one member of her family to concentrate on at a time. The young, beautiful and increasingly glamorous Princess of Wales bore the brunt of media attention in the early '80s. When she could not even go out to buy a packet of wine gums in Tetbury, the village where the Prince and Princess of Wales bought their first home, without the press's telephoto lens being trained on her, the Queen tried to put the brake on.

She had a group of newspaper editors and other media people round to the Palace for a talk about the situation, asking them for restraint. Not much was shown. For a time, the media concentrated their fire on Princess Michael of Kent, then on the marriage of the Princess Royal (the new title given to Princess Anne by the Queen in acknowledgement of the splendid work she did for many charities), then on Miss Sarah Ferguson, the bride of Prince Andrew who had himself figured often in the gossip columns during his days of bachelor freedom.

Sarah Ferguson, whom Prince Andrew had known since childhood, became Duchess of York on her marriage, as the Queen

*Charles and Diana with baby William, 1982*

## FAMILY MILESTONES
### 1982–1992

**June 1982**
Birth of Prince William of Wales, son of the Prince and Princess of Wales

**September 1984**
Birth of Prince Henry of Wales, second son of the Prince and Princess of Wales

**July 1986**
Wedding of Prince Andrew, Duke of York, and Miss Sarah Ferguson

**April 1986**
Death of the Duchess of Windsor

**August 1988**
Birth of Princess Beatrice of York

**March 1990**
Birth of Princess Eugenie of York

*With Edward at Jesus College, Cambridge in 1984*

*Watching the 1985 Derby at Epsom*

made Andrew Duke of York on the morning of his wedding. But it was as 'Fergie' that Andrew's bride was to figure in the tabloid press even more than her husband in the first years of their marriage.

Their first child,

*A mother and daughter heart to heart, 1985*

*Attending a polo match with Charles at Smith's Lawn, Windsor, 1985*

Beatrice, was born in 1988, and their second, Eugenie, in 1990, by which time the media seemed less concerned with reporting the minutiae of the Yorks' family life.

By now, the separation of the Princess Royal and her husband had been announced and accepted, at the time with relatively restrained comment. The princess continued the very busy public life which had earned her much admiration—and, incidentally, earned her charities, especially the Save the Children Fund, huge sums of money and considerable valuable publicity.

Prince Edward, youngest child of the Queen and Prince Philip, also found the searching light of media interest focused on him for a time in the mid-'80s. He had gained a good degree in archaeology and anthropology at Cambridge and had then gone into the Royal Marines. Like Prince Charles, Edward had taken a keen interest in the theatre while at Cambridge; unlike either

*Andrew and Sarah's wedding day. Edward was best man.*

*A portrait of a happy woman, 1987*

of his brothers, he decided that the Action Man life of the forces was not for him and, amidst much press attention, left the Royal Marines. By 1988, he was working in the theatre and has continued to do so while carrying out a regular round of royal engagements.

The 90th birthday of the Queen Mother, the most admired member of the Royal Family after the Queen herself, naturally attracted much interest. She showed little sign of wishing to slow down into a quiet old age. Her engagement diary remained busy, and included trips abroad as well as many events in the UK.

The Queen demonstrated that she did not consider her mother an old lady past enjoying herself by giving a very grand ball in 1990 to mark four family birthdays which fell that year: the Queen Mother's 90th, Princess Margaret's 60th, Princess Anne's 40th and Prince Andrew's 30th. Many members of the Queen's extended family were there to help celebrate the birthdays, and to demonstrate that the Royal Family is a close-knit group.

*The children playing on a fire engine at Sandringham, New Year 1988*

*Outside Clarence House on Mummy's 90th birthday, 4 August 1990*

Edited by Isabel Moore
Designed by Peter Butler

Reproduction by Imago Publishing Limited

All pictures supplied by The
Hulton Picture Company except: title page,
and pages 67 (top), 85 (top), 99, 101,
112, 113, 114, 115, 116, 117 (both), 122, 123 (bottom), 124
Syndication International Ltd.